UBSTANCE
SE, CONCURRENT
ISORDERS
ND GAMBLING
ROBLEMS
N ONTARIO

UBSTANCE
SE, CONCURRENT A
ISORDERS GUIDE FOR
ND GAMBLING HELPING
ROBLEMS PROFESSIONALS
N ONTARIO

Centre for Addiction and Mental Health
Centre de toxicomanie et de santé mentale

Library and Archives Canada Cataloguing in Publication

Substance use, concurrent disorders and gambling problems
in Ontario : a guide for helping professionals.

Includes bibliographical references.
Also available in PDF and HTML formats.
ISBN 978-0-88868-742-5

1. Drug addicts--Counseling of--Ontario. 2. Alcoholics--Counseling
of--Ontario. 3. Gamblers--Counseling of--Ontario. I. Centre for
Addiction and Mental Health

HV5840.C32O57 2008a   362.2909713   C2008-906238-8

ISBN: 978-0-88868-742-5 (PRINT)
ISBN: 978-0-88868-743-2 (PDF)
ISBN: 978-0-88868-744-9 (HTML)
Product code: PZZ93

Printed in Canada

Disponible en francais sous le titre: *Troubles concomitants et problèmes liés à l'usage
de substances et aux jeux de hasard et d'argent en Ontario : Guide pour les professionnels
aidants*

This book was produced by:
Development: Diana Ballon, John Zarebski, CAMH
Editorial: Nick Gamble, Jacquelyn Waller-Vintar, CAMH; Heather Sangster, Strong Finish
Design and typesetting: Mara Korkola, CAMH
Print production: Christine Harris, CAMH

2947a/11-2008/PZZ93

Acknowledgments

Thanks to Andrew Johnson, who first recognized the need for an adapted version of this guide and helped to shape the direction and vision for this new publication. Special thanks are due to John Zarebski, a consultant for CAMH in Chatham, Ontario, who—over a considerable period—generously contributed his ideas on the content and direction of this book and suggested content experts to review the document over two separate phases of its development. Many thanks are due Diana Ballon, whose wordsmithing, sleuthing and true diligence have resulted in a clearly written, concise handbook that should be in every Ontario physician's office and community health centre. Much appreciation is also due to Caroline Hebblethwaite, a publishing developer at CAMH who responded amicably to countless questions lobbed across the hallway. Many thanks to Nick Gamble, who edits with not only an uncannily scrupulous eye for detail, but also a clear vision of larger structural issues, and an obvious love of language.

REVIEWERS

In 2008, the book was reviewed by experts both within and outside CAMH to ensure the accuracy of the information, and its relevance to helping professionals in the field. Many thanks to the following reviewers for their expertise and their willingness to provide input on a document that ideally will influence how helping professionals provide services to clients throughout the province. A very special thanks to Tim Godden and Marilyn Herie, who reviewed several drafts and far exceeded what any reviewer could realistically be expected to provide.

· Susan Allen, co-ordinator, The Family Council, CAMH, Toronto
· Dr. Krishna Balachandra, Concurrent Disorders Program, St. Joseph's Healthcare, Regional Mental Health Care, London
· Larry Corea, director, Drug and Alcohol Treatment Information System, CAMH
· Anne Counter, manager, Information and Referral Services, Drug and Alcohol Registry of Treatment and Ontario Problem Gambling Helpline
· Michael Dean, manager, Addiction Services, St. Joseph's Health Centre, Toronto

· Barry Fellinger, manager, Information and Referral Services, Mental Health Service Information Ontario
· Karen Frayn, director, CONNECT Counselling Services, Canadian Hearing Society
· Tim Godden, advanced practice clinician, Addictions Program, CAMH
· Sylvie Guenther, concurrent disorders priority co-ordinator, CAMH
· Marilyn Herie, project director, TEACH, CAMH
· Greg Howse, executive director, Simcoe Outreach Services, Barrie
· Kathy Kilburn, system consultant, CAMH
· Larry Lalone, addiction education consultant, Organizational Development and Learning Services, St. Joseph's Healthcare, London
· Norma Medulun, regional director, Addiction Services, Niagara Health System
· Robert Murray, manager, Problem Gambling Project, CAMH
· Cheryl Peever, manager, Women's Mental Health Program, CAMH
· Nick Rupcich, manager, Windsor Regional Problem Gambling Services
· Brian Rush, senior scientist and co-section head of the Health Systems Research and Consulting Unit, CAMH
· Wayne Skinner, deputy clinical director, Addictions Program, CAMH
· Brenda Teasell, problem gambling therapist/trainer
· Jon Thompson, director, Riverside Community Counselling Services, Fort Frances
· Karna Trentman, operational supervisor, Information and Referral Services, Drug and Alcohol Registry of Treatment and Ontario Problem Gambling Helpline

The following reviewers provided helpful feedback regarding changes needed to the original *Alcohol and Drug Treatment in Ontario* booklet, first published in 1994. (The organizations listed next to their names reflect their place of employment in 2004, when this review was conducted.) Julia Bloomenfeld, Jean Tweed Centre, Toronto; Michael Dean, St. Joseph's Health Centre, Toronto; Tom deGryp, Salvation Army Correctional and Justice Services; Barbara Everett, Canadian Mental Health Association; Vicente Gannam, Ministry of Health and Long-Term Care; Sonja Grbevski, Windsor Regional Hospital; Kathy Kilburn, CAMH; Greg Howse, Simcoe Outreach Services; Linda Palanek, Niagara Alcohol and Drug Assessment Service; Brian Rush, CAMH; Monique R. Serow, Pinegate Addiction Services,

Sudbury; Linda Sibley, Addiction Services of Thames Valley, London; Susan Smither, CAMH; Carol Strike, CAMH; and Cindy Tanguay, Trenton Military Family Resource Centre.

Contents

SECTION 3: CONCURRENT SUBSTANCE USE AND MENTAL HEALTH PROBLEMS

SECTION 4: PROBLEM GAMBLING

SECTION 5: TREATMENT CHOICES

69   REFERENCES

APPENDICES

Introduction

Why this guide?

A growing number of people who come to health care providers are experiencing not only substance use problems, but gambling and/or mental health issues as well. These problems affect people of all ages, education and income levels, religions and cultures, and in all work situations. Sometimes clients are dealing with just one of these types of problems, but more often than not a person will have more than one of these problems concurrently.

The information in this book is intended to help you determine, when talking with clients, whether someone may need additional counselling or treatment. The book also offers tools to help you to connect with clients about these issues in a way that is empathic and non-judgmental, so that they may eventually seek the help they need.

Helping professionals can make a significant difference in whether people address substance use, gambling and/or mental health problems. Even brief interventions can make a huge difference in people's lives. Because of our overloaded system, non-specialists are—more and more—being called on to help identify, and in some cases treat, people with the kinds of problems described in this book. In many instances, people would not have received the help they needed within the addiction and mental health treatment system if not for the work of dedicated community clinicians and other helping professionals.

People with the kinds of problems described in this book need a wide range of services and supports—not just health and social services, but housing, education, employment and other supports that can't possibly be addressed by one provider. It is the responsibility of helping professionals to work together to help people get the various treatments and supports they are asking for.

This guide was created to help you, as a helping professional, to be aware, sensitive and skilled in screening for these kinds of problems in the clients you see, and to refer people for treatment or, for those with appropriate training, to provide some basic counselling yourself.

An earlier version of this guide was published in 1994 under the title *Alcohol and Drug Treatment in Ontario: A Guide for Helping Professionals.* Feedback on this original guide indicated that it was a valuable resource for helping professionals, but that the material needed to be updated and to include information on how to help identify and, if possible, treat clients with gambling and/or mental health problems as well as substance use problems. *Substance Use, Concurrent Disorders and Gambling Problems in Ontario: A Guide for Helping Professionals* is the product of that feedback. This revised guide provides up-to-date information on the kinds of issues that clients now present to health providers, along with current prevalence statistics and approaches to screening and assessment, as well as treatment options available in Ontario.

Who should read this guide?

This guide will be useful to people working in such fields as:
· health care, addiction services and mental health
· family practice / doctors' offices, community health centres, Aboriginal Health Access Centres, family health teams and Community Care Access Centres
· employee assistance programs
· social services
· child and family services
· correctional services.

We generally refer to people working in these fields as "helping professionals." These are professionals who work in health and social services but who are not necessarily substance use, gambling, mental health or concurrent disorders professionals. They may, for instance, be nurse practitioners, family doctors, social workers, social service workers, probation officers or occupational therapists.

The intended readership for this book is broad, and people will vary in terms of the amount of counselling skills training they have and their level of comfort with providing treatment. For instance, this guide could be equally useful to a family doctor who can prescribe medication and provide counselling or to a settlement or housing worker who may come in contact with someone with a potential addiction or mental health problem while dealing with a non-health-related issue.

How to use this guide

For readers without clinical or counselling training, this book can be used to help identify and screen clients. Those who do have a clinical background will be able to use the information from this book to screen and to begin basic treatment, referring to specialists as necessary. The stages of change model discussed in Sections 2 to 4 can be applied in different ways: a helping professional can use it to help identify the stage the client is at and how motivated the person is to change or, if the professional has a clinical background, he or she can use some of the questions to help explore the problem with the client in more depth and to address the person's ambivalence about change.

It is important to recognize that not only the person with the substance use problem, gambling problem or concurrent disorders may need help. Those living with or otherwise managing the problems of a significant other may also need support. By asking not only screening questions, but also questions about how family members and friends are coping, you will send the message that they too deserve support in their own right.

Reading this introductory section is a good starting point. It highlights the need to be open-minded with clients, recognizing that what they say, how they say it and sometimes what they *don't* say will be influenced by many factors—including the culture with which they identify themselves and the stigma they may have already experienced.

You will likely find that the symptoms and behaviours a client describes reflect multiple causes and that a single problem rarely appears in isolation. The intention of this book is not to provide comprehensive assessment and treatment information, nor to enable you to diagnose; rather, it is to enable you to screen for the various types of problems described in Sections 2 to 4, to provide some basic treatment if you have the clinical background to do so, and to refer the person for further assessment and more specialized treatment if needed. Applying a stages of change model to each of these types of problems will help you to discover where the client is at and how motivated he or she is to address the problem.

While the original guide dealt only with alcohol and other drug problems, this book recognizes that someone may have problems with gambling and/or may have a combination of issues referred to as concurrent disorders—which also requires treatment. By reading each section of this book, you will get a sense of how each type of problem may manifest slightly differently and how clients' care needs become more complex when they are dealing with multiple problems at the same time.

An overview

This guide contains information about how to:
· establish a trusting relationship with clients
· identify people who have problems with substance use or gambling, or who have concurrent disorders
· explore these concerns with clients and encourage them to take action
· connect with ConnexOntario Health Services Information, a gateway to treatment services for alcohol and other drug problems, gambling problems and mental health problems.

The book is arranged in five sections. Section 1 discusses how to build an effective relationship with clients. Sections 2 to 4 follow a similar structure. They begin by providing prevalence statistics that reinforce why you should care about these problems; they define what the problem is (whether a substance use problem, concurrent substance use and mental health problems, or a gambling problem); and they address risk factors and the effects of the problem, how to screen for the problem, and how a stages of change model can be applied to addressing the issue. The final

4

section on treatment offers ways for people to get specialized help.

Section 1: Building a relationship

This section discusses establishing rapport with a client, offers tips for asking difficult questions, and highlights the importance of addressing practical concerns the client might have. It also examines the influence of culture on people's perception of their problems and their willingness to get help, and suggests ways to make services more accessible to people from diverse cultures. Finally, it looks at involving the family in the client's care, and providing support and education to friends and relatives coping with the client's problem.

Section 2: Substance use

This section suggests ways to talk to people about their use of alcohol and other drugs. It presents sample questions to ask, a guide to help you decide whether there is reason to be concerned, a description of how change happens, and ways to build people's motivation to stop or reduce their substance use.

Section 3: Concurrent substance use and mental health problems

Many people who seek treatment for a substance use problem discover they have a mental health problem that also requires treatment. The converse is also true: people with mental health problems are more susceptible to having substance use problems. When substance use and mental health problems are treated together, people tend to have a better outcome. This section will help you to understand the impact of concurrent disorders, and offers tools for screening people with these problems.

Section 4: Problem gambling

This section provides an overview of what problem gambling is, and some of the common behavioural, emotional and health-related signs that may indicate a gambling problem. Also provided are some tips for making gambling something you can more easily talk about with clients. The section provides information on screening tools, risk factors, signs of a gambling problem and how to use a stages of change approach with people who have problems gambling.

Section 5: Treatment choices

This section presents ways to respond when clients are ready to act. It answers common questions about substance use, concurrent disorders and problem gambling treatment, and describes the types of services available in Ontario. It also includes information on ways to support family members who are affected by the client's problems.

It is followed by two appendices:
· Appendix A: Provincial Programs
· Appendix B: CAMH Resources and Publications.

Stigma

Stigma refers to negative attitudes (prejudice) and negative behaviour (discrimination) toward people with substance use or mental health problems (Centre for Addiction and Mental Health, 2007).

Stigmatizing attitudes and behaviours include:
· having fixed ideas and judgments, such as thinking that people with substance use, gambling or mental health problems are not like us; that they caused their own problems; or that they can simply get over their problems if they want to
· using discriminatory or prejudicial language to refer to people with these problems (e.g., "drunks," "junkies")
· not understanding that these are health problems rather than moral failures
· fearing and avoiding what we don't understand—such as excluding people with substance use, gambling or mental health problems from regular parts of life (e.g., from having a job or a safe place to live) (Centre for Addiction and Mental Health, 2007).

Helping professionals, like others in society, can be judgmental or discriminatory toward people with substance use and gambling problems and concurrent disorders. We may, sometimes without even knowing it, have negative thoughts and feelings about people with mental health and addiction problems. As Wayne Skinner explains, these feelings "reflect attitudes that have been formed through the influence of our families, our society, our personal experiences and our own level of understanding" (2005, p. xviii). These negative feelings may manifest themselves as pity, fear, disdain, moralistic attitudes and even contempt.

People who experience stigma often talk about feelings of shame, anxiety, frustration, depression, helplessness, fear and hurt. Over time, they may start to see themselves in terms of the negative stereotypes others have of them, internalizing a sense of hopelessness or shame. This makes it even more difficult for them to talk about their difficulties and any related concerns they may have.

Because mental health and addiction problems carry a particularly negative label in some cultures, certain terms or ways of describing a client's problem may offend the client, depending on the person's own belief systems. For instance, some people may not like to be told they have a "disorder," while others may find comfort in a medical diagnosis. It will be important to explore these belief systems with each client.

One of the best ways to combat stigma and the barriers it creates to people getting help is to confront your own attitudes and beliefs about mental health and addiction problems, so that you can then be open to talking with clients about the difficulties they describe. Being informed about the issues—whether the issue is drugs and their effects, the impact of gambling problems on the family, or having both mental health and substance use problems—will help clients to feel less isolated and more understood. And recognizing and challenging certain stigmatizing beliefs, such as thinking that people with mental health problems are dangerous or creepy, or thinking that people with substance use problems are simply too weak or self-indulgent to change, can go a long way to creating a more empathic response in your work with clients.

Screening

Throughout this book, we offer informal ways to screen clients for the *possibility* of having a substance use, gambling and/or mental health problem. Basic screening tools are *not* meant to elicit a complete profile of a person's psychosocial functioning—that requires a more comprehensive assessment. If you have reason to suspect that the person has one of the problems discussed in this guide, it is important also to screen for the others, given the high prevalence of problems occurring together—either at the same time or at some point in the person's life (once someone has had a problem, there is a risk that the problem may recur).

Screening questions should not focus solely on the person with the mental health and/or addiction problem. Rather, you may also want to ask if the person is living with or otherwise managing the problems of a significant other, to give the message that family members also deserve support in their own right.

When doing an initial screening, you can ask the client a few direct questions, yielding responses that might make you suspect a more significant mental health, substance use or gambling problem. If the client has a positive screen for one or more of these types of problems, a more in-depth assessment by a qualified professional is then recommended, in order to:

· establish a diagnosis
· assess the client's level of psychological functioning
· develop a treatment and support plan that addresses how mental health and substance use difficulties interact and what can be done to address these and any related problems (Health Canada, 2001).

A note about harm reduction

The sections of this guide devoted to substance use and gambling problems reflect a commitment to reducing the negative personal, social and economic consequences of these issues. This approach, often referred to as "harm reduction," does not require people to stop using substances or to refrain from gambling, even though their ultimate goal may be stopping. Rather it presents a range of goals: in the case of substance use, from using substances more safely (e.g., not drinking and driving, not sharing needles) to using less or, if this is the person's goal, stopping altogether; and in the case of gambling problems, setting limits on the amount of time or money spent on gambling, deciding not to gamble when feeling vulnerable, and finding other meaningful activities or other strategies.

A note about language

Substance use

We use the term "substance use" in this book because it is more accurate than the term "drug use." People can have problems with substances that are not drugs per se but that still have mind- or mood-altering effects, including inhalants such as solvents, gasoline and glue. The term also includes prescription and over-the-counter medications, which can cause problems if used inappropriately.

We also use the phrase "alcohol and other drugs" to highlight the fact that alcohol is a drug. In fact, alcohol is the most widely abused drug in our society. Proportionally, the harms and deaths related to alcohol use are far greater than those of all other drugs combined, excluding tobacco. We do distinguish alcohol from other drugs, however, because many people think of alcohol separately from illegal drugs such as marijuana and cocaine.

Concurrent disorders

"Concurrent disorders" is the term used in Ontario to refer to mental health and substance use problems that co-occur, either at the same time or at different times, and in different intensities and forms over a person's lifetime. It is thus the term we use in this book for these co-occurring problems.

Addiction

The term "addiction" is used when referring to both substance use and gambling problems. We do not use the term if we are referring to only one of these problems separate from the other.

Building a relationship

To ask the kinds of screening questions suggested in this guide requires a positive, trusting relationship between the client and the helping professional. Many people may never have opened up to a health professional. Others may have discussed certain difficulties they are having—such as problems sleeping, arguments with a spouse or stress at work—without identifying a possible underlying mental health and/or addiction problem.

In this section, we discuss the necessary steps for helping professionals who talk about difficult subjects with their clients.

Establishing rapport

Shame, embarrassment or fear of disclosure may keep people from revealing substance use, mental health or gambling problems. By being respectful and interested in the client's life and explaining that your questions are routine—and the answers confidential—you will help the person feel more comfortable and open to discussing his or her concerns. Only by identifying these problems can you then help the person to find the treatment or support needed.

Here are some basic steps to building a rapport, many of which are principles of motivational interviewing (see page 39):

· Ensure the person is comfortable.

· Emphasize that the questions are routine and the answers confidential.

· Express empathy. This involves demonstrating respect and interest in the client's hopes and goals, and accepting what the client says, even if you don't necessarily agree with it (Sagorksy & Skinner, 2005). (You may need to explain the subtle distinction between accepting and agreeing.)

· Look for barriers to understanding—such as language, culture, education, physical or mental challenges—and accommodate the barriers as best you can (e.g., get a translator, get information about the specific cultural group).

· Roll with resistance. In other words, expect clients to resist the idea that they might have a problem that needs to change, and recognize that this does not mean the client is not motivated to change (Sagorksy & Skinner, 2005). Avoid arguing with clients. In the case of substance use and gambling, provide objective information about what is "normal" as a standard against which they can gauge their own behaviour. Talk about the typical impacts of problems like these. Acknowledge the challenges of making changes.

· Support self-efficacy. This involves believing in the client's ability to change, and pointing out any successes, however small, that the client has made.

Asking the difficult questions

It is important to ensure that a client who has a mental health and/or addiction problem is identified, so that the person has the potential to get the treatment he or she needs.

· Make it a routine practice to talk about substance use, gambling and mental health with every person seeking help.

· Be aware that many people with one of these types of problems also have others.

· With people identified as being at risk, ask follow-up questions at future interviews.

· Be mindful of the language you use, taking into account the burden of stigma carried by people with substance use and gambling problems and concurrent disorders (see the information on stigma on page 6 and language on page 9).

Addressing immediate concerns

Clients with more than one mental health and/or addiction problem, and those with more severe and persistent problems, will likely also have significant difficulties in other aspects of life (e.g., work, housing, relationships, physical health). You may need to provide practical support for these more immediate concerns before addressing treatment for the addiction and/or mental health problem. For instance, if a client tells you that he or she has just been evicted or has not been able to see a doctor because of a lost OHIP card, you could refer the person to other sources of support or help the person to draw on existing ones (e.g., the support of a close family member or a friend).

If any part of your discussion raises concerns about the client's safety or the safety of anyone connected to the client (such as a parent or child), address these concerns first. (For a list of support services, see Appendix A.)

Providing culturally sensitive care

It is important to consider the influence of culture on how people seek help, the kinds of feelings and attitudes each person has toward his or her illness and the suggested treatment, and the meanings he or she ascribes to terms such as "illness" and "treatment." Do not assume that all people from a certain culture hold certain shared beliefs, values and norms; instead, ask about the person's experience of illness and what kind of support they find helpful (Kleinman & Benson, 2006). Keep in mind too that the term "culture" refers not only to a person's racial identity and ethnicity, but also to other aspects of identity such as religion, gender, sexual orientation, profession, region and disability status (Substance Abuse and Mental Health Services Agency, 2003).

Research suggests that people from certain cultural communities are less likely to get the care they need because of such barriers as language, discrimination, stigmatizing attitudes and "mistrust of mainstream service providers." Some people may be more likely to conceal problems they see as shameful until health or financial problems, loss of a job or a family crisis forces the issue into the open (Agic, 2004).

Having respect for different traditions, health beliefs and practices is essential to developing effective programs for culturally diverse communities.

In part, this means making direct efforts to consider how accessible your services are to people from diverse backgrounds. This includes:

· learning about the racial, cultural and ethnic backgrounds of the populations you serve, and familiarizing yourself with one or two of these groups that you encounter most often

· translating your brochures and forms, or providing other ways to ensure that health messages are relevant and appropriate (e.g., through discussion, visual images)

· having trained interpreters available for clients (note that you are obliged, under the Canadian Charter of Rights, to bring in a certified American Sign Language interpreter for a signing deaf person; you can book one through Ontario Interpreter Services or through the Canadian Hearing Society website at www.chs.ca)

· asking what the person calls the problem he or she is experiencing

· making referrals or recommendations based on the kinds of support the client identifies as helpful (Substance Abuse and Mental Health Services Agency, 2003).

Involving the family

For every person with an addiction or mental health problem, many more are affected, both in finding help for the individual and in coping with and managing their own lives. Depending on the person's culture, he or she may define family narrowly in terms of the nuclear family or more broadly as the extended family, which could even include neighbours and close friends (Chang & Kelly, 2007).

While clients are increasingly being involved in their own care, family members also need support, information and education about their family member's condition. You may want to ask clients about the impact their problem is having on the family, and offer support to help family members cope with the effect their relative's condition is having on them.

Many families are under great stress. They may be having difficulty coping, they may be arguing a lot, and relationships may be strained. If the person with the problem is a parent, the children may feel forgotten, neglected, depressed, angry or even as though they are to blame for their parent's problem. Or the problem may have been so mired in secrecy that children will sense something is wrong but not know what it is. Children need some explanation and support, geared to their age, to help them understand the parent's problem. (For books on how to talk to children about some of these problems, see *Wishes and Worries: A Story to Help Children Understand a Parent Who Drinks Too Much Alcohol* [CAMH, 2005] and *Can I Catch It Like a Cold? A Story to Help Children Understand a Parent's Depression* [CAMH, 2002], listed in Appendix B.)

It can be helpful for family members to have input into treatment planning, but this kind of participation must be agreed on by the person with the problem. As the helping professional, you should ask the client if he or she wants to have family members involved in planning and treatment (O'Grady & Skinner, 2007).

For information on supporting family members, see page 66 in Section 5, "Treatment Choices."

Substance use

Why we should care

· In 2006/07, there were 81,782 new admissions to specialized services for substance use treatment in Ontario. Sixty-eight per cent were men and 32 per cent women—a slight increase in the proportion of women over the previous three years (Drug and Alcohol Treatment Information System, 2008).
· In a Canadian study conducted in 2002, just under 10 per cent of those surveyed reported alcohol problems in the last 12 months, including about two per cent who met criteria for dependence. During the same period, three per cent reported illicit drug use problems, including about one per cent who met criteria for dependence (Rush, Urbanoski et al., 2008)

Types of substance use

Substance use can involve using any of the following. When you are talking to clients about substance use, you can explain the terms used by giving examples:

Alcohol	beer, wine, coolers, liquor
Prescription drugs	amphetamines ("uppers" or "speed"), barbiturates

	("sleeping pills"), opioids ("painkillers," OxyContin), steroids, benzodiazepines ("benzos," "tranks," "downers")
Over-the-counter drugs	Gravol, painkillers with codeine, cough syrup, antihistamines
Illegal drugs	cannabis (marijuana, hashish) (other than marijuana prescribed to treat serious illness), cocaine ("coke," "crack"), heroin, hallucinogens (LSD or "acid," mescaline, PCP), ecstasy ("E"), methamphetamine ("crystal meth," "Tina"), GHB ("G," "liquid ecstasy"), ketamine ("special K")
Inhalants or solvents	glue, gasoline, paint thinner
Tobacco	cigarettes, pipes, snuff, Snus, chewing tobacco, shisha (water pipe), cigars, cigarillos, herbal cigarettes, bidis (small, hand-rolled cigarettes)

The popularity and availability of drugs, as well as their street names, change constantly. The Centre for Addiction and Mental Health (CAMH), or a local addiction treatment service, will have the current facts about alcohol and other drugs. CAMH's *Do you know…* pamphlet series provides information on a variety of substances of abuse and their effects. (See Appendix B for a list of substances in this series.)

How to screen for substance use problems

· Begin with a question to explore the person's past substance use or use a general screening tool such as the CAGE-AID (see page 21) to determine whether the problem requires further assessment.
· If the person has used alcohol or other drugs, ask about current use.
· If there is current use, ask about any concerns caused by use in the past year.
· Ask about tobacco use, as people with substance use problems often smoke (Selby & Herie, in press). About 80 to 90 per cent of people who are dependent on alcohol, 80 per cent of people who use cocaine and 90

per cent of people who use opiates also use tobacco (Perkins et al., as cited in Selby & Herie, in press).

· Decide if there is reason to be concerned, based on your observations and the client's answers to your questions.

· Use the following sample questions to help you phrase questions that suit your own style, your work environment and the person you are talking to. You can preface these questions with a comment such as "I'm asking questions to help raise your awareness of where you stand," as people may not realize that they have entered a risky level of substance use.

Sample Questions

ALCOHOL USE

· How often do you have a drink containing alcohol?
· How many drinks containing alcohol do you have on a typical day when you are drinking?
· Are there times when you drink more than this?
· What negative consequences have resulted from your use of alcohol?

PRESCRIPTION DRUG USE

· Have you ever used a prescription drug (e.g., painkiller, sleeping pill)? How often have you done this in the past year? Have you used someone else's prescription?
· For medications prescribed by your doctor, have you ever used more of the medication or used it more often than you were instructed to? Have you ever used if for a reason other than the one for which it was prescribed? Have you ever obtained a prescription for the same drug from more than one doctor? What questions or concerns do you have about prescription drugs?

OVER-THE-COUNTER DRUG USE

· What over-the-counter drugs have you used in the past year? What were they used for? How much did you use? How often? For how long?
· What positive and/or negative effects have you experienced from using an over-the-counter drug?

ILLEGAL DRUG OR INHALANT USE

· Have you ever used illegal drugs (e.g., unprescribed cannabis, cocaine, heroin)? How often have you done this in the past year? How much?
· Have you ever used an inhalant (e.g., glue, gasoline, paint thinner) to get "high"? How often have you done this in the past year?
· Are there any concerns or questions you have about drugs or inhalants?

TOBACCO

· Do you ever smoke [tobacco] or have you ever smoked regularly?

· If currently smoking: How long after waking up do you have your first cigarette of the day? (Less than 30 minutes denotes severe dependence.)

· How many cigarettes do you smoke per day? What about other tobacco products? (Explore current and past use.)

The following guidelines will give you clues about the client's alcohol use and may require you to ask more detailed questions.

Low-Risk Drinking Guidelines

There may be reason to be concerned about a client's alcohol use when responses reveal a pattern of drinking that regularly exceeds the low-risk drinking guidelines. This includes drinking more than two standard drinks on any day and:

· if male, consuming more than 14 drinks per week

· if female, consuming more than nine drinks per week.

Low-risk drinking guidelines have been developed by a team of medical and social researchers who consider both the harms associated with alcohol, especially when consumed in large quantities, and the beneficial aspects of alcohol, especially when used in moderation. (Alcohol should be avoided altogether by people with certain health problems, women who are pregnant, and people at particular risk of developing a problem related to alcohol use.)

One standard drink = 13.6 g of alcohol:

· 5 oz. / 142 mL of wine (10–12% alcohol)

· 1.5 oz. / 43 mL of spirits (40% alcohol)

· 12 oz. / 341 mL of regular strength beer (5% alcohol).

Note that the concept of a standard drink will vary in different communities. The term may be confusing and foreign in communities where people don't measure or count drinks and/or where the alcohol content of drinks is unknown (Agic, 2004). Higher-alcohol beers and coolers have more alcohol than one standard drink.

For more information about the low-risk drinking guidelines, see www.camh.net.

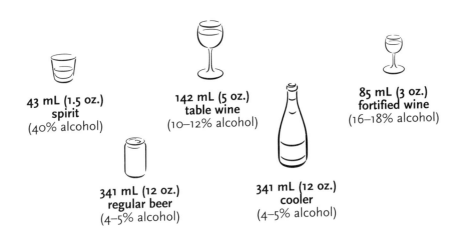

43 mL (1.5 oz.)
spirit
(40% alcohol)

142 mL (5 oz.)
table wine
(10–12% alcohol)

85 mL (3 oz.)
fortified wine
(16–18% alcohol)

341 mL (12 oz.)
regular beer
(4–5% alcohol)

341 mL (12 oz.)
cooler
(4–5% alcohol)

SCREENING TOOLS

If, after discussing the client's substance use, you are concerned about his or her use of a specific substance or several substances, there are various screening tools that can help provide more information. These include the CAGE-AID (the CAGE questionnaire Adapted to Include Drugs), provided below, and the Fagerstrom Test for Nicotine Dependence (Heatherton et al., 1991).

The CAGE-AID is a simple tool to screen for alcohol and other drug use problems. It was adapted from the original CAGE, which was designed to detect problem drinking.

CAGE-AID

The CAGE-AID is a four-item screening tool:

· Have you ever thought you ought to **C**ut down on your drinking or [other] drug use?
· Have people **A**nnoyed you by criticizing your drinking or [other] drug use?
· Have you felt bad or **G**uilty about your drinking or [other] drug use?
· Have you ever had a drink or used [other] drugs first thing in the morning to steady your nerves or to get rid of a hangover (**E**ye-opener)?

A score of two or more "yes" answers = a positive CAGE and further evaluation is indicated.

Source: Reprinted with permission. Brown, R.L., & Rounds, L.A. (1995). Conjoint screening questionnaires for alcohol and drug abuse. *Wisconsin Medical Journal 94*, 135–140.

If you do identify possible substance use problems, it is also important to screen for any accompanying mental health and gambling problems. For more information about screening for concurrent disorders, refer to page 36 in Section 3. For information on screening for problem gambling, see page 48 in Section 4.

Knowing when to be concerned

Without jumping to conclusions, there may be reasons to be concerned about other forms of substance use when someone's responses reveal:

· use of a prescription drug not prescribed for that person
· use of a prescription drug in amounts exceeding those set by the prescriber
· use of a prescription drug through inappropriate routes (e.g., injecting or inhaling rather than taking orally)
· obtaining the same prescription drug from more than one doctor
· combining different drugs, including combining alcohol with other substances
· any use of illegal drugs or inhalants.

Other reasons for concern are questions or comments that reveal the client is:

· using over-the-counter drugs, such as Gravol or medicines with codeine, in quantities higher than recommended on the product label or for reasons other than indicated for the product (e.g., using Gravol as a sleeping medication)
· missing work, school, court dates or family events because of alcohol or other drugs
· risking conflict with the law because of alcohol or other drug use (e.g., driving a car, motorboat or snowmobile while impaired or using illegal drugs)
· using alcohol or other substances of abuse while pregnant
· operating equipment while intoxicated (e.g., heavy equipment at work, a stove, lawn mower or power tools at home).

Warning signs

The following chart will help you identify early warning signs of substance use, along with more serious problems. Warning signs mean that harms are likely if a person's substance use isn't eventually addressed; serious problems are those in which immediate action is needed to address serious risks to the person's well-being.

Warning Signs and Signs of More Serious Problems

PROBLEM AREA	WARNING SIGNS	SIGNS OF SERIOUS PROBLEMS
Psychological/emotional	forgetting things, feeling concerned or worried about drinking	depression, feeling hopeless or worthless, personality changes, thoughts about suicide, suicide attempt
Family	quarrels, neglecting responsibilities, cutting down on family activities or outings because of substance use	divorce, partner abuse, child abuse or neglect, being excluded from family events
Work, school or home	lower performance, missing work, lower grades, cutting classes, wanting to be alone much of the time	accidents at work, falls or accidents at home, job loss, suspension from school, quitting school
Financial or legal	spending too much on alcohol or other drugs, recklessness, verbal aggression	driving while or after using alcohol or other drugs, problem gambling, debt, stealing, loss of driving licence, assault, incarceration for substance-related problems

continued on next page

PROBLEM AREA	WARNING SIGNS	SIGNS OF SERIOUS PROBLEMS
Health	falls or other minor accidents, misuse of other drugs (over-the-counter, prescription and illegal), stomach problems, disrupted sleep, shakiness or dizziness, fatigue	using alcohol or other drugs while pregnant, changes in cognitive functioning, ulcer, gastritis, liver disease, strokes, overdose, abnormal heart rhythm, diabetes, memory loss, blackouts

Responding when substance use problems are unlikely

When there is no cause for concern about substance use:
· make information about alcohol and other drugs available as part of routine practice: present information in a non-dramatic way, as a prevention strategy (e.g., "Research has shown that it can be harmful for men to drink more than two drinks on any day, and more than 14 drinks in a week.")
· encourage the client to raise any concerns or questions that might arise in the future
· ask questions about substance use if something comes up in a session that raises a red flag, or if there is sufficient time (i.e., one year or longer) between client contacts that a reassessment is warranted.

There is probably no cause for concern when the client is:
· drinking moderately in accordance with the low-risk guidelines
· in regular contact with one family doctor for prescription drug use, is using prescription drugs infrequently and as prescribed, and has no concerns about prescription drugs
· occasionally experimenting with one of the less addictive drugs such as marijuana or has done so in the past, and the client—as well as others in the person's life (e.g., teachers, family members, employers)—has no concerns about illegal drugs or inhalants. (However, there are some substances, such as solvents, that can bring about serious negative effects – in some instances,

death – with only a single use. Therefore, it there is any doubt about a person's health being compromised by any substance use, it would be important to consult with a medical professional as soon as possible.)

Discussing and acting on concerns

It is important to take a safety first approach: if your discussion has raised concerns about the client's safety or the safety of anyone connected with the person (e.g., the partner, child), address this concern first.

Encourage an open and objective discussion of concerns by identifying which stage of change the client is experiencing and by responding appropriately, as described on the following pages. Avoid directing the client to take specific action-oriented steps until his or her concerns and ambivalence about change have been explored. Also avoid labelling the client in any way (e.g., as an "alcoholic" or "drug addict"), since this may make the person feel more defensive or blamed.

Whether the client's goal is to cut down or to stop substance use, emphasize that no one should ever stop using multiple substances at once without professional help (especially in the case of certain addictive drugs), as this can be dangerous and even life-threatening.

If the person smokes, discuss the importance of addressing his or her tobacco use, and point out that the long-term effects of smoking can cause even more harm than other types of substance use. The person may choose to address a smoking problem while in treatment for other substance use problems or may choose to treat the two problems separately. While some studies show that the early relapse rate for a substance use problem can be higher if treated concurrently with a tobacco use problem, sometimes addressing them both at the same time can be helpful (Selby & Herie, in press).

Make the person aware of the advantages of acting earlier:
· People who address their substance use early on have a better chance of a full recovery. Early problems do not need to develop into serious problems.
· Intervening early means that treatment will be briefer and can more likely be arranged around work, school and family routines.
· Chronic substance use problems tend to be more serious and require more intensive treatment.

Identifying which "stage of change" the client is experiencing

Change is rarely sudden. Rather than occurring in one transformative moment, it happens in stages (Hester & Miller, 2003).

The stages of change model can be used to help assess how ready a client is to make a change, so that you can determine the best way to work with the client, based on how motivated he or she is (Sagorsky & Skinner, 2005). The following description of change reveals how some people seeking help respond quickly when a concern is identified, while others may not perceive their substance use as a problem. For example, a client may come to you with anxiety, and—with further questioning—you discover that he is consuming eight alcoholic drinks a day. The client may not see the connection between his alcohol consumption and the anxiety, nor recognize that he is drinking too much. (For more about concurrent disorders, see Section 3.) Helping professionals who can anticipate a client's response are better able to encourage action and obtain help for people who need to change their substance use.

People experience change differently. People may:
· move through the stages of change either quickly or slowly
· remain "stuck" in one stage
· skip or repeat stages.

Prochaska and DiClemente (1984) have identified six stages of change (see the table below).

Stages of Change

PRECONTEMPLATION STAGE

The person is not considering change and does not recognize the need for change: "Yes, I drink. I like drinking."

The person is surprised by concern of family members or co-workers: "I can't understand why they are upset."

The person may resist attempts to explore concerns or may deny there are problems: "I definitely don't have a problem with drugs. It's just a once-in-a-while thing. I can quit anytime."
"My alcohol consumption does not have anything to do with my anxiety."

CONTEMPLATION STAGE

The person is considering change:

"Yes, I've thought about cutting down."

The person is not ready to commit to change:

"But I enjoy it too."

"Maybe my alcohol consumption has something to do with my anxiety."

PREPARATION STAGE

The person is getting ready to change:

"I'm sick of being in and out of shelters. It's time for me to get a real life."

"If I were to cut down on my weed, do you think that would get my parents off my back?"

"I love my smokes, but maybe I need to cut back a bit."

"I hate what I've done to my family. It's time to take a hard look at some of the choices I've made in my life."

ACTION STAGE

The person has initiated change:

"I've decided to go for treatment. Where can I get in?"

"I am ready to talk about cutting down on my drinking in the hopes of lessening my anxiety. I also need to find a therapist."

The person expresses urgency:

"I just need a telephone number."

MAINTENANCE STAGE

The person is adjusting to change:

"I'm taking it one step at a time."

The person is acquiring and practising new skills and behaviours:

"I went to a movie with my family last night instead of going to the bar."

RELAPSE

The person has begun to slip back into old patterns:

"I saw my drinking buddies the other night."

"My anxiety is back and I have started drinking a lot again to try to calm down."

Building motivation to make changes

When the client is not concerned but the professional is, the objective is to get the client thinking about change or ready to change.

A BRIEF STRATEGY, BASED ON FRAMES

To support the client in moving from earlier to later stages of change, consider using a brief intervention model referred to as FRAMES, an acronym for:

· **Feedback** about risk (giving clients feedback about their risk of having a substance use problem)

· **Responsibility** for change (emphasizing that clients ultimately decide when and how they will reduce or stop their substance use)

· **Advice** (after asking permission to do so, providing non-judgmental advice to clients about ways to change, such as following low-risk drinking guidelines)

· **Menu** of alternative options (offering a range of strategies for ways clients can cut down or stop their substance use)

· **Empathic** approach (being warm and understanding rather than confrontational)

· **Self-efficacy** (encouraging clients to believe in their own ability to change) (Miller & Sanchez, 1994).

FRAMES is one way of motivating clients to make a change. Another is motivational interviewing, which can be used in conjunction with FRAMES. Essentially, it involves "drawing out the client's own motivation to change" (Sagorsky & Skinner, 2005, p. 86). For instance, rather than being confrontational about someone's substance use, you can focus on empathizing with the person, and recognizing and supporting his or her ability to make change.

HELPING TO REMOVE BARRIERS TO CHANGE

When both the client and the professional are concerned, but the client is not ready to change, the objective is to encourage the client to move toward the action stage of change by removing barriers to change. The following are some examples of how this can be done:

- If a client is reluctant to call a contact you have provided because "there is no time," you may want to non-judgmentally reflect back your observation that she is finding it hard to follow through with a plan. This observation can give the person the message that you understand that change is not a simple process. It can also open the door to discussing feelings of shame, guilt and hopelessness that may be keeping the person stuck.
- If someone thinks that change will create money problems, calculate how much money could be saved by quitting or cutting down on drinking and the smoking that accompanies it. (For instance, going on the patch costs about the same as a package of cigarettes. How much does it cost the person to drink what he or she has been consuming each week?)
- If a person believes there is no help for his or her family members, let the person know that ConnexOntario Health Services Information is an excellent resource for this type of information (see page 55).
- If a client is afraid that his or her employer will not understand, explain that many companies have programs that support getting help.
- If someone is concerned about child care, you can let the person know that some early childhood development programs do offer some form of child care.

Exploring the positive and negative aspects of substance use

Looking at the pros and cons is a good way to address someone's ambivalence about substance use because it helps the person to arrive at his or her own decisions about continuing to use, rather than imposing your own judgment or perspective (Sagorsky & Skinner, 2005). It is really about looking at the costs of continued substance use and the benefits to stopping or reducing use.

POSITIVE ASPECTS OF SUBSTANCE USE

By exploring the positive aspects of substance use with clients, you will help them to recognize what motivated them to start using and/or continue. If there were no positive aspects, the person would probably have addressed the problem before.

The *positive* aspects are usually the more immediate effects of the substance use. The following are reasons people often give:

- to cope with unwelcome feelings: this could mean temporarily escaping feelings of stress, depression, loneliness, anger or boredom, or warding off a sense of

worthlessness or shame. (In some cases, it could be to deal with a mental health issue. See Section 3, "Concurrent Substance Use and Mental Health Problems," for a discussion of how to address the link between mental health and substance use problems.)
· to experience pleasure: the person may enjoy the "buzz" or rush they get from the drug, as well as its taste
· to ward off physical pain or help to get rid of hangovers or cravings
· to cope with the effects of trauma, such as flashbacks, anxiety, sleep problems and relationship difficulties (*Bridging Responses: A Front-Line Worker's Guide to Supporting Women Who Have Post-Traumatic Stress* [Centre for Addiction and Mental Health, 2001] provides more information on this topic.)
· to cope with situations: to be less shy or socially inhibited, to show affection or emotions more easily, to have sex, to get to sleep, to be more assertive, to fit in at celebrations where drinking is common or even expected
· out of habit: after work or school, when socializing or with lunch or dinner, as a social outlet.

Even when people can identify the positive effects of a substance, recognizing their motivations may still be a challenge. It is likely that many factors have contributed to a person's substance use. For instance, someone may have started to use and then developed a physical dependence, so that she then finds it too hard to quit even though she would like to.

NEGATIVE ASPECTS OF SUBSTANCE USE

The negative aspects of substance use are covered in the chart "Warning Signs and Signs of More Serious Problems" on page 23. The diagram shows how people who drink and take other drugs may have difficulties in other areas of their lives, such as:
· psychological problems
· problems with family, work, school, money or the law
· problems with their physical health. (Most often, health problems are what prompt people to come to a helping professional. For instance, a client may have diabetes, cardiovascular disease or cancer in addition to his problematic substance use; the substance use may have exacerbated the physical illness or, conversely, the physical illness may have made him more disposed to developing a substance use problem. Learning about each client's lifestyle and overall health will help you to gauge whether he or she is at greater risk of substance use problems.)

People may be more likely to think of the negative aspects of their behaviour when they understand how habits form. The diagram below shows why people continue to do things that cause problems for them: the "pluses" reward continued use by being immediate, expected and familiar, while the "minuses" don't usually happen (or aren't usually apparent) for some time. The negative consequences are in a sense "hidden from view" by the positive consequences.

Use the diagram to help the person see that:
· immediate consequences are mostly positive
· serious negative consequences are mostly delayed
· positive consequences "hide the view" of the negative consequences that may occur down the road.

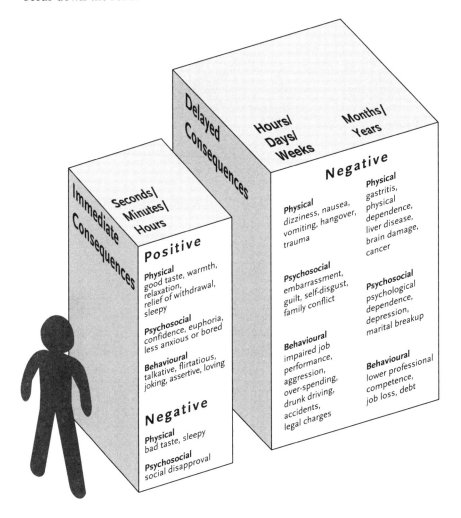

Strengthening commitment to change

After a client has shown that he or she is motivated to make a change, the next step is to strengthen this commitment. The following are some examples of how you could do this:

· When people prefer to change on their own, offer to help them by following up and responding to questions as best you can. People may wish to buy the self-help guide *DrinkWise: How to Quit Drinking or Cut Down* or *Addiction: An Information Guide*, both published by CAMH (the information guide is also available online at www.camh.net). They may also choose to join a self-help / mutual aid group, such as Alcoholics Anonymous or Women for Sobriety, or to access online support (see Appendix A for a list of online counselling, support, self-assessment and self-help resources).

· When people say they are afraid to get help, let them know that you can help them find out what treatment will be like by getting information on the programs that are available (see Section 5, "Treatment Choices"). Considering treatment options also involves exploring what the person might change and how.

· Encourage the client to talk about the situations and circumstances in which he or she uses substances in a way that causes problems (i.e., the places, times and people with whom the person uses).

· Summarize the problems discussed during the interview and give feedback using FRAMES (see page 28).

· Provide feedback about risk (e.g., if there are a lot of problems; if the problems have been going on for a long time; if the problems are creating physical, psychological/emotional, social or behavioural risks for the person).

· Clearly recommend or suggest that the person reduce use or stop altogether. For example, you might say, "Ultimately, it's your call about what you'll do, but if you're looking for my advice, I think you should take a break from drinking for at least a short time."

HELPING CLIENTS TO IDENTIFY OPTIONS FOR CHANGE

You can help clients to:

· set goals (i.e., either to quit or cut down)
· determine timing (e.g., to start cutting down now, next week or this weekend)
· outline what steps they will take (e.g., exercising instead of drinking, doing fun or useful things with people who do not drink or take other drugs, joining a self-help / mutual-aid group, reading a self-help book, finding one of the treatment options discussed in this guide)
· explore treatment options (see Section 5, "Treatment Choices," for information on contacting ConnexOntario Health Services Information to learn where a client can get an assessment).

ACTION AND MAINTENANCE

When the client is ready to act, your objective is to invite movement toward the maintenance stage of change. If the person has made, and is adjusting to, change, you should encourage him or her to remain in the maintenance stage. You can do this by:

· encouraging the client's commitment to change
· supporting the client in assuming responsibility for change
· helping the client to become more confident in his or her ability to change
· suggesting two or more ways to accomplish or maintain change.

These steps will be considered more fully in Section 5, "Treatment Choices."

RELAPSE

When clients relapse (or "slip"), it is important to work with them in a way that guards against feelings of failure and encourages more efforts toward change.

When people relapse, the objective is to help them get back on track quickly. Help them recognize that they are still adjusting to a big change in their lives. They are acquiring and practising new skills and ways of handling situations in which they might have used substances in the past. While they may feel discouraged, they should know that relapse is not uncommon—

and it is not a reason to give up. Help them to recommit to the belief that they can attain the goal they set for themselves, whether this was abstinence or reducing the harms associated with their substance use (including reducing the amount and frequency of use). If a person has recommitted to his or her goal of controlling substance use, you can refer to the relapse as a "slip," affirming the person's efforts in preventing a longer relapse and emphasizing the perspective that all is not lost. However long the relapse lasts, encourage the person to use it as an opportunity to learn why it happened and how to avoid or lessen the triggers, to reduce the chance of a similar slip in the future.

Portions of this substance use section were adapted from *Alcohol and Drug Treatment in Ontario: A Guide for Helping Professionals* (2000).

Concurrent substance use and mental health problems

Why we should care

- The likelihood of having a mental health problem is significantly higher among people with a substance use problem, just as the likelihood of having a substance use problem is significantly higher among people with mental health problems. In addition, the term "concurrent disorders" seldom means having a single mental health issue combined with problems with a single substance. Rather, people often have multiple substance use and/or mental health problems: this is the rule, rather than the exception.
- People with mental health problems are two to three times more likely to smoke than people without mental health problems (Kessler, 1994). People with several mental illness, such as schizophrenia, are even more likely to smoke: as many as 45 to 88 per cent of this population smoke, compared to the general population (Kalman et al., 2005).
- According to population surveys, between 35 and 50 per cent of people with a mental health or substance use disorder do not seek services to treat

their problem (Urbanoski et al., 2008).
· People with concurrent disorders are at greater risk of health and social problems, including homelessness, HIV infection, victimization and domestic violence (Health Canada, 2001).

Understanding concurrent disorders

Treatment providers often refer to co-occurring substance use and mental health problems as "concurrent disorders." These problems can occur at the same time or at different points in people's lives, and in different intensities. People can also have different combinations of concurrent disorders. For example, they might have:
· a drinking problem and an anxiety disorder, perhaps following abuse in childhood
· depression and an addiction to sleeping pills, with accompanying alcohol use
· schizophrenia and tobacco use
· borderline personality disorder, post-traumatic stress disorder, cocaine use and a gambling problem.

How to screen for concurrent disorders

If you have reason to suspect that a person has either a mental health or a substance use problem, it is important to screen for the other type of problem, given the high prevalence of the two occurring together.

When doing an initial screening, you could use an informal checklist to observe certain qualities in the client, or you may ask the client a few direct questions that might reveal the possibility of a more significant mental health or substance use problem (Centre for Addiction and Mental Health, 2006).

SUBSTANCE USE SCREENING

To screen for alcohol and other drug problems, see pages 18 in Section 2, "Substance Use," and the CAGE-AID, page 21.

MENTAL HEALTH SCREENING

There are various ways to screen for a mental health problem, depending on the depth you wish to go into. Approaches range from observing how the person is doing, to asking a few direct questions, to applying more formal screening tools.

Mental health checklist

The following checklist can be used to quickly assess the client's mental health through observation.

ABC Model for Psychiatric Screening

APPEARANCE, ALERTNESS, AFFECT AND ANXIETY
Appearance: General appearance, hygiene and dress.
Alertness: What is the level of consciousness?
Affect: Elation or depression: gestures, facial expression and speech.
Anxiety: Is the individual nervous, phobic or panicky?

BEHAVIOUR
Movements: Rate (hyperactive, hypoactive, abrupt or constant?).
Organization: Coherent and goal-oriented?
Purpose: Bizarre, stereotypical, dangerous or impulsive?
Speech: Rate, organization, coherence and content.

COGNITION
Orientation: Person, place, time and condition
Calculation: Memory and simple tasks
Reasoning: Insight, judgment, problem solving
Coherence: Incoherent ideas, delusions and hallucinations?

(Source: Centre for Substance Abuse Treatment. *Assessment and Treatment of Patients with Coexisting Mental Illness and Alcohol and Other Drug Abuse.* Treatment Improving Protocol [TIP] Series 9. DHHS Publication No. [SMA] 05-3992. Rockville, MD: Substance Abuse and Metnal Health Services Administration, 1994.)

Asking a few questions

You can ask a few direct questions, such as those listed below, if you want more information but would rather not use a more formal screening tool. If the client answers yes to one or more questions, further screening and possibly assessment is needed.

Questions about Mental Health

Have you ever been given a mental health diagnosis by a qualified professional? (yes/no)

Have you ever been hospitalized for a mental health–related problem? (yes/no)

Have you ever harmed yourself or thought about harming yourself, but not as a direct result of substance use? (yes/no)

(Adapted from Health Canada, 2001, p. 37)

Even when answered truthfully, these three questions will still fail to identify many people with concurrent disorders, especially those with less severe mental health problems. However, in settings where more sophisticated screening instruments are not available, asking these three general questions is better than not asking any questions at all.

SCREENING FOR CONCURRENT DISORDERS

You may also want to use more open-ended questions to learn about interactions between a person's substance use and mental health problems (Sagorsky & Skinner, 2005). The GAIN-SS and the PDSQ (see below) are two tools for screening for both mental health and substance use problems. As well, there are specialized tools for the different types of mental health problems—including attention-deficit/hyperactivity disorder (ADHD), obsessive-compulsive disorder, depression and schizophrenia—and for the different types of substance use problems. (*Treating Concurrent Disorders: A Guide for Counsellors* [Skinner, 2005] provides a useful summary and compendium of screening and assessment tools in Chapter 2, Appendix 1.)

The GAIN-SS (**Global Appraisal of Individual Needs—Short Screener**) is a 20-question tool that looks at four different areas: mood and anxiety issues (or internalized problems); behavioural issues (or externalized problems); alcohol and other drugs; and crime and violence. It takes only five minutes to administer, and can be used with both adolescents and adults. Versions in both English and Spanish can be accessed free of charge through the Chestnut Health Systems website at www.chestnut.org. (The only cost involved is a nominal fee for the training software, which is also available through the website and gives you unlimited use.)

The PDSQ (**Psychiatric Diagnostic Screening Tool**) is another tool that screens for the most common Axis 1 psychiatric disorders (e.g., various forms of depression, anxiety, alcohol and drug abuse and dependence, and psychosis). It can be purchased through Western Psychological Services (www.wpspublish.com) and other sources.

The MMR (**Modified Mini Screen**) is a 22-question tool used to identify adults who may need a more intense mental health assessment. It covers three types of mental health problems: mood, anxiety and psychotic disorders. The MMR is available at www.nyc.gov/html/doh/downloads/pdf/qi/qi-mms-scoringsht.pdf. The MMR user guide is available at www.nyc.gov/html/doh/downloads/pdf/qi/qi-mms-userguide.pdf.

Building motivation to make changes

While motivational interviewing and identifying stages of change were originally used for people with substance use problems (see page 28 in Section 2, "Substance Use," for more about how to apply the FRAMES model to work with the client), these approaches have since been found to work well with people who have concurrent disorders.

There are many aspects of motivational interviewing (MI) and the stages of change approach that make it appropriate to use with this population (Sagorsky & Skinner, 2005). MI:

· uses a non-confrontational approach that emphasizes an empathic understanding of the client's concerns and problems
· addresses the person's ambivalence about changing and normalizes ambivalence (e.g., with people who have mental health problems and for

whom substance use may have been a way of coping with other stresses and difficulties)
· focuses on building the person's self-esteem and self-efficacy, which is especially important when—because of the complexity of treating multiple symptoms of concurrent disorders—other treatment approaches may have failed, and the client may be less optimistic about the possibility of change
· can be used to facilitate many behavioural changes (e.g., cutting down on substance use, taking prescribed medication and attending scheduled appointments) or can be adapted to focus on making one small change at a time
· involves acknowledging and respecting the client's goals and hopes, which can include making practical changes (e.g., finding paid work, getting an apartment, working out, upgrading skills), being flexible about change, and often focusing on short-term or immediate goals rather than solely pursuing set, long-term goals
· helps establish a respectful relationship between client and helping professional, which is crucial to the long-term work often needed with people with more complex problems.

ADAPTING MOTIVATIONAL INTERVIEWING FOR PEOPLE WITH CONCURRENT PSYCHOTIC DISORDERS AND SUBSTANCE USE PROBLEMS

Motivational interviewing can also be adapted for work with clients with concurrent psychotic disorders (e.g., schizophrenia) and substance use problems (Martino et al., as cited in Sagorsky & Skinner, 2005). This can be done by:
· asking clear and simple open-ended questions about how the person's substance use and mental health problems interact
· accommodating cognitive difficulties (e.g., difficulties with paying attention, concentrating, organizing information, short-term memory) by, for instance, using repetition, visual aids and concrete language and by taking more breaks during sessions
· using metaphors to help the client understand how change can be helpful (e.g., illustrating the concept of recovery as a three-legged stool, with each leg representing a behaviour, such as taking medication, attending

appointments with the health practitioner and staying abstinent from substance use: when one leg is missing or broken, the stool tips over, resulting in relapse or hospitalization)

· reflecting back to the client reality-based material, rather than the psychotic or delusional material the client may be presenting.

Problem gambling

Why we should care

· According to a 2005 study, the highest rates of gambling problems are found among young adults. Almost seven per cent of 18- to 24-year-olds in the study had moderate to severe gambling problems (Wiebe et al., 2006).
· Over the past 10 years, there has been a significant increase in problem gambling among women. While women have historically earned less than men, they still have many ways to access money, making them just as likely to gamble.
· Only one in 10 people with severe gambling problems gets any type of treatment services (Cunningham, 2005). However, many people with gambling problems are helped in other settings, such as through credit counselling, primary health care, criminal justice agencies and pastoral counselling.
· Rates of "pathological gambling" are six times higher in people with an alcohol use disorder and 4.4 times higher among people who have had any drug use disorder in their lifetime (Rush et al., 2008). (Pathological gambling is a severe gambling problem that seriously harms all aspects of the person's life: the person is unable to control urges to gamble and is more likely to gamble as a way to escape problems and relieve anxiety.)

Understanding what problem gambling is

A person is gambling whenever he or she takes the chance of losing money or something of value and when winning or losing is decided mostly by chance.

Gambling becomes a problem when a person has a pattern of gambling behaviour that may involve more than losing money: it can affect all aspects of the person's world—from personal or family life to work or school, finances and even health.

As opportunities to gamble have increased rapidly in recent years, there has been a rise in problem gambling. People gamble in many different ways, including:

· buying lottery tickets (including charity lotteries)
· playing poker and other card games for money
· betting on sports events (e.g., horse races)
· Internet gambling
· playing casino games
· playing bingo
· playing keno (a bingo-like or lottery-like gambling game)
· using slot machines
· speculating on the stock market (Centre for Addiction and Mental Health, 2005).

While most people can gamble without experiencing problems (either by choosing not to gamble or by betting only what they can afford to lose), some people become preoccupied with gambling and find they are unable to control the amount of time or money they devote to gambling.

Recognizing the impact of a gambling problem

People with gambling problems can be affected in numerous ways, including:
· serious financial loss
· work- and school-related problems

· higher rates of emotional or health problems (including depression, anxiety and substance use problems), which could also have contributed to the gambling problem, as well as resulting from it
· higher rates of suicide
· greater likelihood of marital and family breakdown
· involvement in illegal activities to support their gambling.

Because problem gambling can be hidden for a long time, families may be shocked when the full impact of the gambling loss is discovered. Family members can be severely affected by the gambling, and may come to helping professionals suffering from stress and/or relationship and financial problems. Partners may feel they can no longer trust someone who has been hiding a gambling problem, while the people who gamble may avoid those they love because they feel ashamed. Many families find themselves under significant stress and have trouble coping. When the person who gambles is a parent or caregiver, children can often end up feeling forgotten, neglected, depressed and angry (Centre for Addiction and Mental Health, 2005).

Knowing who's at risk

Certain risk factors can contribute to people developing gambling problems or finding it more difficult to stop. For instance, people are more at risk if they:
· have an early big win (leading to false expectations of future wins)
· have easy access to their preferred form of gambling
· hold mistaken beliefs about the odds of winning
· have had a recent loss or change, such as a divorce, job loss, retirement or death of a loved one
· often feel bored or lonely, or have a history of risk-taking or impulsive behaviour
· have few interests or hobbies, or feel their lives lack direction
· have or have had a history of mental health problems, particularly depression and anxiety
· have or have had problems with alcohol or other drugs, gambling or overspending
· have a parent who has, or has had, problems with gambling
· have been abused or traumatized

· tie their self-esteem to gambling wins or losses
· link their self-esteem to their financial worth.

Research into gambling problems suggests that some groups may be at greater risk of developing problems or may experience greater harm because of their gambling problem (Centre for Addiction and Mental Health, 2005).

Youth are twice as likely as adults to have gambling problems. Easy access to gambling, its wide acceptance as a way to have fun, the perception that it is a quick way to a good life and the element of risk make gambling attractive to teens. Problem gambling in teens is correlated with poor academic and vocational performance, mental health problems, substance use problems and high-risk behaviour.

While older adults and others with low incomes are less likely to gamble, those who develop gambling problems often face more serious consequences because they lack the financial resources to replace losses.

Groups that are often marginalized (e.g., new immigrants, Aboriginal people) may also be at increased risk for developing gambling problems because of the stresses they confront. Both groups encounter isolation, poverty and racism, while each group also faces specific challenges. Aboriginal people often confront the loss of culture and language, while newcomers to Canada often have to deal with the stress of immigration, weakened social and family relations, financial difficulties, employment challenges, language and cultural barriers and a desire to achieve rapid financial success. Cultural factors shape beliefs about money and gambling; these beliefs need to be asked about, understood and factored into your relationship with the person seeking your help (Centre for Addiction and Mental Health, 2005).

Recognizing the signs of a possible gambling problem

Gambling problems share many similarities with other addictive disorders and with mental health problems. Here are some common signs of problem gambling you may identify in clients (Centre for Addiction and Mental Health, 2005). You may see one or two of these signs in people who do not have a gambling problem, but when someone exhibits a large number of signs—and an overall pattern of problems—the possibility that gambling is a problem requiring formal support should be explored.

BEHAVIOURAL SIGNS

The person:
· spends a lot of time on gambling-related behaviours, such as studying sports statistics or racing forms, or visiting casinos
· thinks and talks excessively about gambling
· stops doing things he or she previously enjoyed
· misses family events
· changes patterns of eating, sleeping or sex
· ignores self-care, work, school or family responsibilities
· is absent for long, unexplained periods of time
· uses alcohol or other drugs more often
· leaves children alone, seems less concerned about who looks after them, neglects their basic care
· has legal problems related to gambling.

EMOTIONAL SIGNS

The person:
· withdraws from family and friends
· seems emotionally detached or anxious, or has difficulty paying attention
· has mood swings and sudden outbursts of anger
· becomes secretive and/or irritable about money matters
· complains of boredom or restlessness
· seems depressed or suicidal.

HEALTH SIGNS

The person complains of stress-related health problems, such as:
· headaches
· stomach and bowel problems
· difficulty sleeping
· overeating or loss of appetite.

FINANCIAL SIGNS

The person:

· frequently borrows money or asks for salary advances
· takes a second job without appearing to have extra money
· cashes in savings accounts, RRSPs or insurance plans
· hides bank and credit card statements, doesn't pay bills and is being called by creditors
· has conflicts with other people over money
· is less willing to spend money on things other than gambling
· cheats or steals to get the money to gamble or pay debts
· alternates between having no money and having a lot of money.

How to screen for gambling problems

It is rarely helpful to ask a person directly, "Are you having a problem with gambling?" Some people may not have insight into how their problems are related to gambling. For others, a blunt approach may produce a defensive response and leave the person unwilling to explore the issue further.

There are, however, numerous ways to ask about gambling as a routine part of interacting with clients:

· Ask about recreational activities: "What do you do for fun? Do you go to the movies, clubs or the racetrack?" "Do you ever go to casinos or other places to gamble?" In phrasing questions, avoid communicating a moral judgment; assume that the person does participate in some type of gambling: "How often do you buy lottery tickets?"
· Ask, "How much time and money do you spend on these activities?" You may find it difficult to ask clients how they spend their money if you are not used to it. Many North Americans believe it is rude to ask other people about money and spending. You can assure clients that problems with gambling are common and that you ask everyone you work with how much of their time and money is devoted to gambling (Centre for Addiction and Mental Health, 2005).

SCREENING TOOLS

If, after discussing gambling, you are concerned that a client may have a problem, there are several screening tools that can provide more in-depth information about the person's problem. As a helping professional, you are in a position to identify people who may be experiencing problems with gambling, to support their efforts to change, and to connect them to problem gambling resources.

Here are three screening tools. The first two can be downloaded from the website www.problemgambling.ca (as can a longer seven-item version of the five-item CAMH Gambling Screen).

· **Canadian Problem Gambling Index (CPGI) Short Form:** a nine-item tool (condensed from the original 31-item questionnaire) that clients can use to assess their own gambling, or that you as the helping professional can use.

· **Check Your Gambling:** a screening tool that people can complete online. By responding to the questions, people can get immediate results that provide feedback about how their gambling compares to others', and offers recommendations for next steps. This kind of information has been shown to have a positive effect on people's motivation to address their gambling. Clients can complete it for themselves and can also e-mail the results to you.

· **CAMH Gambling Screen:** a quick, five-item screen to help identify people who may have a gambling problem but are not getting treatment:

CAMH Gambling Screen

1. In the past 12 months, have you gambled more than you intended to?
❒ Yes   ❒ No

2. In the past 12 months, have you claimed to be winning money when you were not?
❒ Yes   ❒ No

3. In the past 12 months, have you felt guilty about the way you gamble or about what happens when you gamble?
❒ Yes   ❒ No

4. In the past 12 months, have people criticized your gambling?
❒ Yes   ❒ No

5. In the past 12 months, have you had money arguments that centred on gambling?
❒ Yes   ❒ No

Two or more "yes" responses indicate that there may be a problem with gambling and that the person should be referred for further assessment.

(Source: Turner, N. & Horbay, R. [1998]. *The* CAMH *Screen: An Unpublished Screening Tool Based on the South Oaks Gambling Screen.*)

Another approach to screening for gambling problems is to screen for risk factors that are associated with these problems, such as anxiety, depression, erroneous beliefs and impulsivity. (A concurrent disorder—particularly depression and anxiety is very common with a gambling problem. For more on concurrent disorders, see Section 3, "Concurrent Substance Use and Mental Health Problems.")

Tools that specifically measure pathological gambling in adolescents include the South Oaks Gambling Screen – RA (SOGS-RA)—downloadable from www.problemgambling.ca—and the *Diagnostic and Statistical Manual, Version IV*, Juvenile Criteria (DSM-IV Junior).

A tool, also available at www.problemgambling.ca, that can help clients to better understand their gambling is the **Self-Monitoring Gambling or Urges to Gamble** tool. This allows people to track and record the circumstances in which they gamble (e.g., when, what type of gambling, their mood at the time, the time spent, whether they won or lost) to help them recognize gambling patterns and understand triggers and coping strategies.

Navigating the stages of change

As with substance use problems and concurrent disorders, clients with gambling problems go through various stages of change that reflect their motivation to address the problem. (For a more detailed description of stages of change, see pages 26–27 in Section 2, "Substance Use.")

People with a gambling problem are unlikely to progress through the stages of change model in a linear process. Rather, gambling counsellors describe clients as moving through the various stages in a more complex, cyclical process that is highly influenced by the unpredictable win/loss experience associated with gambling. For example, many clients move from a contemplation phase to an action phase very quickly, and miss the preparation stage altogether. Others may impulsively stop gambling after a heavy loss, ban themselves from the casino and manage to completely sustain this change without every having planned and prepared for a lasting change. Still others may move back to a contemplation or precontemplation phase from whatever stage they were in, if they suddenly have a win that holds out the promise of a larger win. If they do have a big win, this may change the perception of their gambling as a problem. In fact, a big win early on is a strong predictor of someone developing a gambling problem, as are intermittent wins.

Some adolescents who gamble may be particularly prone to moving through these stages in a cyclical or circuitous way, while others may be able to move through the stages quite quickly, supported by parental example and other aids (DiClemente et al., 2000).

Building motivation to make changes

Getting the client to think about change is an important aspect of the helping professional's role. You can help guide clients to their own conclusions by using FRAMES (see page 28 in Section 2, "Substance Use") or by following the motivational principles outlined on pages 11–12 in Section 1, "Building a Relationship" and when adapted for people with concurrent disorders on page 39 in Section 3.

PRECONTEMPLATION

If the client is not considering change and doesn't recognize there is a problem, point out the impact gambling is having on his or her life. Or encourage the client to reflect on why others may think there is a problem. At this stage, it is important to educate the client or raise his or her awareness of the problem or the potential for one. You could provide financial facts that the person can use to measure his or her own gambling behaviour. For instance, "Financial planners tell us that we should be spending four to five per cent of our income on entertainment."

With clients at this stage, begin a non-judgmental exploration of where the problem is at—with the hope of creating a bit of tension that will move the person into the contemplation stage. (See the description of FRAMES in Section 2, page 28, for a guide on how to work with people using this model.)

You can also recommend that clients use the Self-Monitoring Gambling or Urges to Gamble tool to help track their gambling and the CPGI-Short Form to assess whether they have a problem that needs to be addressed.

CONTEMPLATION

If the person is considering change, help him or her to weigh the positive and negative aspects of continuing gambling versus at least reducing the amount of time and money devoted to the activity. Provide information about problem gambling services and explore potential barriers to accessing these services. Help clients to explore possible solutions to problems they have identified. And use the Self-Monitoring Gambling or Urges to Gamble tool or CPGI-Short Form if you think they could be useful.

PREPARATION

This is a crucial stage for clients to plan and prepare how to change their gambling behaviour. At this point, they should have a goal they feel is important and achievable. You could ask clients how they will increase their odds at succeeding or how they will make it impossible to fail at the goals they have set. Helping clients to recognize triggers and urges to gamble is an important preventative strategy.

ACTION

While effort is being made, reaching this stage does not mean that the person has changed yet. Implementing a plan for change is not always easy. Not only do people with gambling problems need to deal with their triggers and urges, they may also need to mend broken relationships, look at how they are going to manage their debt, and eventually learn how to manage their money. Sometimes people will return to the contemplation stage and struggle with their goal decision. If this happens, you can repeat the pros-and-cons exercise. If someone is committed to change, link the person to the appropriate services. (See page 60 in Section 5, "Treatment Choices.")

MAINTENANCE

If the person is adjusting to change, help him or her develop strategies to maintain the change. Be encouraging, while acknowledging that slips can happen. Help the person to develop skills to prevent relapse. The maintenance stage can be a vulnerable time for relapse to occur. Often, the person is getting less attention from friends and family members. The crisis is over and the person seems to be doing well, so others may think the problem is gone. The person with the gambling problem may believe the same thing.

RELAPSE

For many people trying to deal with their gambling problem, relapse is a part of the process. Should a slip or relapse occur, the client may be back at the contemplation stage. People with a gambling problem may cycle through the stages quickly again, depending on whether they win or lose.

For information about treatment, see the next section.

Involving the family

While issues pertaining to the family are addressed in Section 1, "Building a Relationship," and Section 5, "Treatment Choices," gambling problems have financial implications for families that warrant a separate discussion here. Consider including a client's children, partner or other family members in your discussions (if the client agrees), or arrange to meet with the family separately. Often family members are more willing to discuss the impact of gambling than the person who gambles. Your assessment of a client's gambling problem may be based on what a family member tells you.

Recognize that discussing the family's situation can be an agonizing experience for the person who gambles and his or her partner. This may be the first time the client has acknowledged the extent of the problem, and gambling can have a significant financial effect that is felt by the entire family. The partner may respond with a loss of trust and significant anger and frustration that may be a challenge for you to navigate in your meetings.

While family members may want to help by paying off debts, you may want to discuss how this approach can be risky: it can send the message that if the client returns to gambling, someone will bail him or her out, thereby enabling the gambling to continue. Encourage families to take steps to protect their assets from further loss with the help of a financial counsellor, and refer them for legal advice, if needed. (For information on credit and debt counsellors, clients and family members can contact the Ontario Problem Gambling Helpline; see Appendix A.)

Treatment choices

Your first contact: ConnexOntario Health Services Information

When looking for treatment for a client, contact ConnexOntario Health Services Information (www.connexontario.ca) as a first step to finding the appropriate services. ConnexOntario offers three information services— the Drug and Alcohol Registry of Treatment (DART), the Ontario Problem Gambling Helpline (OPGH) (with interpretation available in more than 140 languages) and Mental Health Service Information Ontario (MHSIO). Each provides information and service referrals in Ontario, available 24 hours a day, seven days a week. You outline the problem(s) the client is experiencing and any constraints (such as mobility or geography), and a professional referral agent tells you what services are available. Clients can also call themselves, as can a concerned friend or family member. Calls are free, confidential and anonymous. In addition, each service has a searchable online directory of services.

· Drug and Alcohol Registry of Treatment
  1 800 565-8603
· Ontario Problem Gambling Helpline
  1 888 230-3505

· Mental Health Service Information Ontario
1 866 531-2600
· For a list of provincial programs, see Appendix A.

Preparing for treatment

As a helping professional interested in supporting a person in the change process, it's also important to be aware of pacing. Even though a person has experienced many negative consequences, he or she may still not be convinced that now is the time for action. If a well-intentioned counsellor gives into the temptation to insist on immediate cessation of the problem behaviour, the result can be to drive the person away. In other words, the counsellor's insistence that the client must stop a behaviour right away can be one of the barriers to a person's chances of achieving abstinence in the long term (Miller & Page, 1991).

Your role in preparing the client to begin treatment is to:
· give information that helps the person make a choice about treatment
· ask the person to think about his or her choices and discuss them with family or friends who have their best interests at heart
· encourage the person to name, explore or envision his or her own reasons for making a change, noting that change may involve not only reducing substance use or seeking treatment for a mental health problem and/or addiction, but also achieving practical goals, such as continuing school, finding a job, securing low-cost housing, or going to a family doctor about a physical health problem)
· Help the person to identify the two or three main reasons for seeking treatment to address his or her problem—for example, to save an important relationship; to improve health and fitness; to save money for a family holiday.
· Have the person identify the positive outcomes of change—a good relationship, a healthy body, a happy holiday. Help the person keep these images vividly in mind.
· Help the person make the first appointment.
· Offer them the companion to this guide—a brochure directed to clients called *Substance Use, Concurrent Disorders and Gambling Problems: A Guide for People Seeking Help in Ontario*
· Develop the person's confidence in his or her ability to get better and even

recover: point out that nearly every person with addiction and/or mental health problems has setbacks (someone with a cocaine addiction may try to stop many times before finally succeeding, in the same way that someone might have recurring episodes of a mental health problem before treatment helps to reduce the frequency or severity of episodes). Follow up in future interviews with praise and encouragement for any small success.

Answering common questions about treatment

HOW CAN THE CLIENT ACCESS TREATMENT?

This section provides information on getting treatment, either for a person with a substance use, gambling and/or mental health problem. (For more information on accessing services for family members or friends who are supporting the person, see "Supporting Family Members," page 66.)

There may be waiting lists for many services, and specialized care is often limited. Some services (e.g., case management) may not be readily available; in many such cases, a therapist or counsellor may try to fulfil this important function.

Substance use

There are two ways for clients to enter the system:
· by going through initial assessment / treatment planning
· by entering withdrawal management.

The process of initial assessment / treatment planning:
· provides up-to-date information about alcohol and other drugs
· helps people understand the risks associated with their substance use, including its effect on others
· encourages people to begin the process of change
· helps people arrange appointments, admissions, etc., as needed
· matches people to the services they need, such as:
  - *community services*: once referred to as "outpatient," these services range in intensity from brief counselling to structured day or evening programs

(e.g., specialized concurrent disorders treatment) and more intense programs (e.g., every day or several times a week) for substance use, gambling and related problems

- *residential services*: these services include residential treatment services; residential medical / psychiatric services (available for more severe problems); and residential supportive treatment services (once referred to as "recovery homes"), which provide less structured, less intensive care (not necessarily staffed 24 hours a day, seven days a week), often used by people before or after a more intensive residential program.

People may enter the treatment system via *withdrawal management* (once referred to as "detox") if they need support to withdraw from substance use where the withdrawal has physical effects. Stopping some drugs without professional help can be dangerous, particularly when multiple substances are involved. (A small percentage of people will require more intensive medical care to withdraw.) Withdrawal management is for people who are intoxicated, in withdrawal or in crisis due to their substance use.

Withdrawal management services are available either in the community (for people withdrawing from a substance while living at home or in a residential supportive setting) or in a withdrawal management centre. There are three levels of withdrawal management services, from Level 1 (the least intensive) to Level 3, which is for people requiring medically assisted withdrawal. Some areas offer day withdrawal management services and telephone supported withdrawal management services.

You or the client can call ConnexOntario's Drug and Alcohol Registry of Treatment to find out about which services are the most appropriate and nearest to the client's home. For more information on substance use services in Ontario, see www.dart.on.ca or contact 1 800 565-8603.

DO SUBSTANCE USE SERVICES HAVE ADMISSION AND DISCHARGE CRITERIA?

Staff in substance use treatment agencies follow standard admission and discharge criteria to match each client to the most appropriate treatment.

Concurrent disorders

It can be particularly complicated to identify and treat two or more problems that don't necessarily have a clear connection (Skinner, 2005). Research clearly shows that clients do better and the system saves time and money when treatment for concurrent disorders is integrated and co-ordinated—that is, when clients' mental health and substance use problems are addressed together.

If this cannot be done in one location, then a case manager (or counsellor or therapist, if there is no designated person to fulfil this role) can help to co-ordinate the client's treatment, so that all health professionals involved know what is being done to treat various aspects of the client's difficulties. Case management is critical in helping clients—particularly those with complex, multiple issues—to navigate different service systems and programs, and to advocate on their behalf where needed. Sometimes it makes sense to treat one problem first (e.g., a drinking problem may be treated before a concurrent mood disorder, or a mental health problem that is getting worse may be treated before a concurrent substance use problem) (Skinner et al., 2004).

Clients can get help for concurrent disorders by connecting with ConnexOntario's DART (1 800 565-8603) or Mental Health Service Information Ontario (MHSIO) (1 866 531-2600). They may be directed to a designated concurrent disorders program or they may have to access mental health and substance use treatment separately. DART can help you to locate community or residential treatment options for people with concurrent disorders, though there may be waiting lists, particularly for residential programs.

The criteria are designed to put the person first and to encourage agencies to focus on meeting clients' needs, rather than fitting clients into available services. By using these criteria, treatment agencies ensure that people are referred to the appropriate level, intensity and type of care throughout their treatment.

Definitions of the provincial service categories within the substance use treatment system are available through www.dart.on.ca.

MENTAL HEALTH

Accessing mental health care services can be challenging. With no fixed point of entry and no standardized assessment, clients begin the road to recovery from a variety of venues. They may enter the system through a hospital emergency room or mobile crisis service after a psychotic episode, suicide attempt, unfortunate run-in with the police or other crisis; through the criminal justice system; or after a visit to a family doctor (if the person is fortunate enough to have one). A family doctor could prescribe psychotropic medication and/or offer basic counselling or, if the person requires more in-depth therapy or specialized medication consultation, could consult with or refer the client to a specialist, most likely a psychiatrist.

Because of these multiple entry points, knowing where to go can be confusing for professionals and clients alike. ConnexOntario's MHSIO (1 866 531-2600) provides information on a wide variety of mental health services funded by the Ministry of Health and Long-Term Care, not only concurrent disorders treatment programs, but:

· counselling and treatment programs
· supportive and supported housing
· assertive community treatment (ACT) teams
· crisis services and short-term crisis support beds
· family initiatives and consumer/survivor groups
· social rehabilitation and vocational programs
· abuse services.

Less detailed information is available on services for less severe, more common problems. For instance, someone looking for a family doctor or psychiatrist will be referred to the College of Physicians and Surgeons, while a person seeking a therapist in private practice will be referred to the relevant governing body, such as the Ontario Psychological Association or the Ontario College of Social Workers. MHSIO may also refer you or the client directly to a community health centre (which may, for instance, have a psychiatrist on staff part-time) or a family health team.

Family members seeking support or information can access support groups run through the Canadian Mental Health Association, the Schizophrenia Society of Ontario or the Mood Disorders Association of Ontario. Family members of people with hearing problems will be referred to CONNECT. (See Appendix A for more information on how to reach these organizations directly.) You can also refer to *Challenges and Choices: Finding Mental Health Services in Ontario* (CAMH, 2003) for more detailed information about various types of mental health problems, getting an assessment, finding a therapist, accessing community supports, getting help in a crisis and taking medications.

Problem gambling

Clients can access gambling services simply by connecting with the appropriate community treatment service in their area. They don't necessarily have to go through initial assessment / treatment planning first, as they do for substance use problems. Rather, most community services will offer assessment and community treatment counselling in-house and will connect the client to more intensive options, such as residential treatment, for more serious issues. Substance use and gambling services are often provided through the same agency. The province uses a portion of gambling revenues to fund treatment for gambling in communities across Ontario.

Treatment options include:

· community treatment, which may involve individual counselling or meeting with a group for one or two hours a week

· more intensive community treatment, which involves structured programs offered both in the day and evening, and often involves meeting for three hours a day, up to five days a week, to help the person develop the skills needed to control his or her gambling

· residential treatment for people who require even more intensive services (there are three residential treatment programs for problem gambling in Ontario: two are for both men and women while the third is for women only).

For more information on problem gambling treatment resources, see www.opgh.on.ca or contact the Ontario Problem Gambling Helpline at 1 888 230-3505.

WHAT ABOUT OTHER DIFFICULTIES THAT CAN'T BE ADDRESSED DIRECTLY BY AN ADDICTION OR MENTAL HEALTH COUNSELLOR?

Often, mental health, substance use and/or gambling problems will have created other difficulties in a client's life, particularly when the person is seeking help for co-occurring problems. For instance, people with concurrent disorders may need help in areas such as housing and employment, while people who gamble may need legal advice and referrals to financial services. Clients may also have physical health problems that have arisen as a result of other difficulties in their lives. Families may need to access family or couple therapy, psychoeducational groups or other support systems. For a listing of provincial services, see Appendix A.

WHAT KIND OF APPROACH TO TREATMENT CAN THE CLIENT EXPECT?

Problem gambling and substance use counsellors typically use similar strategies: a cognitive-behavioural approach with harm reduction or abstinence goals. Treatment may also include social skills training, medication supports (e.g., Antabuse, methadone), psychoeducational groups (groups that provide information about the addiction), coping skills, problem solving, relapse prevention, connection to mutual aid groups such as Alcoholics Anonymous, Women for Sobriety, Gamblers Anonymous or other strategies as needed.

Treatment for concurrent disorders includes psychosocial treatment (psychoeducation, psychotherapy, family therapy and peer support) and/or medication. Psychotherapy can be short (usually no more than 10 to 20 sessions) or long (generally at least a year). It can involve cognitive-behavioural therapy (CBT), which addresses the person's thoughts and feelings; dialectical behaviour therapy, which incorporates CBT practices with mindfulness training and practice; psychodynamic therapy, which focuses more on gaining insight into longer-term issues; and interpersonal therapy, which looks at how people communicate and relate to one another (Skinner et al., 2004).

Therapy may involve the family as well as the individual.

WHO CAN MAKE A REFERRAL TO FORMAL TREATMENT OR OTHER SUPPORT SERVICES?

Many services accept referrals from any source, without requiring a note from a doctor or other health care professional. Although clients can—and most commonly do—refer themselves to many support services, it is helpful, whenever possible, for the client to have a family doctor or other community health care professional involved in his or her care. This is because there are many potentially helpful services in the treatment system—particularly for people with multiple problems—that are available only if the client is seeing a doctor or other community professional who can help co-ordinate the overall treatment plan. Using a "consultation model," treatment agency staff works with the client, providing a specialized assessment and set treatment recommendations in a similar way to specialists in physical health care practice. With the help of a community health professional, a person may, for instance, be able to get a medical assessment from a doctor to make him or her eligible for an inpatient addiction program, or get support to implement part of the treatment plan after the client has been discharged.

Even clients without a family doctor should be encouraged to seek support within the treatment system so they can be matched to services that are available. If a family doctor or other community health professional is required for a referral to a specialized service, the client can be supported in making this arrangement while participating in a program that is immediately accessible.

At times, you may want to help the client book an appointment to create a more seamless entry into the treatment system. Note that people will likely require an assessment before being accepted into a residential program.

WHO CAN MAKE A REFERRAL TO SELF-HELP OR MUTUAL AID GROUPS?

Mutual aid groups such as Alcoholics Anonymous (AA) can be accessed at any time by anyone. The only admission requirement for 12-step groups such as AA, Narcotics Anonymous, Cocaine Anonymous or Gamblers Anonymous is a desire to stop (or in some cases reduce) one's substance use or gambling. While up-to-date information about specific meetings places and times is not always available, contact information for groups in a specific area is available from many sources including the Internet, family physicians, local newspapers, food banks, ConnexOntario and the phone book.

For information on self-help groups for people with depression or bipolar disorder, contact the Mood Disorders Association of Ontario. For information on self-help groups for people with schizophrenia, contact the Schizophrenia Society of Ontario. For information on finding other self-help groups in the province, contact the Self-Help Resource Centre, the Ontario Self-Help Network or the Canadian Mental Health Association (see Appendix A for contact information).

Peer support groups are available to help family members and friends cope, stop blaming themselves for their loved one's problems and focus on their own health and well-being. For instance, for gambling problems, family members can join Gam-Anon or (if they are teenagers) Gam-Ateen; for alcohol problems, they can join Al-Anon, Alateen or Adult Children of Alcoholics; and for alcohol and/or other drugs, they can join Parents against Drugs (PAD).

Internet self-help groups are also available. See Appendix A for more details.

CAN ONTARIO'S SERVICES ADDRESS THE NEEDS OF CLIENTS FROM DIVERSE POPULATIONS?

Wherever possible, agencies tailor their services to meet specialized needs needs or the needs of people from particular cultural backgrounds. Some agencies specialize in treating a specific population group or offer a range of specialized programs (e.g., treatment groups for women, older adults or people who are using a particular substance; services that make special provisions for people with disabilities, or that provide services in languages other than French and English, and in a culturally affirming way).

Programs for special populations include those operated by:
· the National Native Alcohol and Drug Abuse Program (NNADAP), which helps Aboriginal people and their reserve communities establish and operate programs aimed at reducing high levels of alcohol and other drug problems, including solvent abuse (see www.hc-sc.gc.ca/fnih-spni/substan/ads/nnadap-pnlaada_e.html)
· the Canadian Hearing Society, which offers assessment and counselling services on mental health and addiction issues for people who are deaf, deafened and hard of hearing (see www.chs.ca/en/counselling.html).

See Appendix A for more details on these and other programs.

However, some more specialized services are not available in all communities, and the ones that do exist may not meet everyone's needs. For instance, CONNECT—a small, community-based general mental health and addiction service for all people who are deaf, deafened and hard of hearing—isn't able to refer clients to more specialized services because they simply don't exist for this population. Even self-help groups that are available may feel isolating to someone who is the only deaf person in a group of hearing people. At the same time, some people may shy away from groups with other deaf people for reasons of anonymity or confidentiality.

ConnexOntario has information on these agencies and programs.

WHAT DOES IT COST?

There is no charge for many addiction services in Ontario, as they are funded through the Ministry of Health and Long-Term Care. Accessing some services requires a valid health card. If a client does not have an OHIP card but is eligible to receive one, help the person make getting a health card a priority.

Certain services have associated fees (e.g., the cost to fill a prescription for methadone, some residential treatment, some legal and financial services for people with gambling problems or their families, and certain types of psychotherapy). While psychotherapy from a general practitioner or psychiatrist is free, therapy from psychologists, social workers and other health practitioners is not covered unless their services are provided through hospitals, community agencies (excluding family service agencies), the client's workplace employment assistance program or certain private clinics. Their fees may be partly covered under extended health insurance plans, the Workplace Safety and Insurance Board or other private insurance companies. Some psychotherapists do offer a sliding scale (reduced rates suited to the person's income).

ConnexOntario only provides information on programs funded by the provincial government, so private practitioners who work on a fee-for-service basis (e.g., certain types of counsellors/therapists) are not listed.

There are no dues or fees for joining self-help / mutual aid groups. Some of them are government funded, while others support themselves through voluntary contributions from members.

WHAT WORKS IN TREATMENT?

Research indicates that:
· no single treatment approach works for all people
· one of the most important factors for the success of psychotherapy is a trusting relationship with an empathic therapist; this is at least as important as the type of therapy being used
· co-occurring problems are an expectation, rather than an exception
· continuous, integrated treatment, with one person or team overseeing the client's care, is crucial, particularly when working with people who have

concurrent disorders or people with the most severe mental health and/or addiction issues
· brief interventions may be all that is needed: they are more effective than no treatment, and may be as effective as more intensive treatment for people with mild to moderate substance use problems
· addressing underlying life problems can improve treatment outcomes (although people can address problem behaviours before they fully understand "why" the problem exists)
· considering the influence of gender, race, age and/or life stage in the client's life is important in nurturing a respectful relationship with the client that focuses on sustaining life changes the person has identified as significant.

Evidence suggests that the most effective service for a client will be one that:
· addresses the client's needs, rather than the perspectives of the helping professional
· supports the client's strengths
· is preferred by the client.

Treatment decisions need to be reconsidered when:
· the client does not follow the plan of care
· the client is dissatisfied
· the client does not respond well to treatment
· the care does not address what the client has identified as major concerns in his or her life.

To maintain your connection with the client:
· ask about the progress of treatment
· praise all successes, however small, in a genuine way
· encourage the client to keep going
· should relapse occur, reassure the person and support his or her continued efforts to change
· at the end of your time together, let the person know how to reconnect if he or she feels vulnerable or experiences a slip or relapse.

Supporting family members

As with any health problem, many more people are affected by a substance use problem, concurrent disorders or a gambling problem than simply the person who seeks treatment. Family members and friends are playing an increasing role in the care of loved ones, particularly when the problem is chronic or when there are co-occurring problems that exacerbate the person's difficulties with coping. In some cases, though, family members may not get involved or seek support until a crisis forces them to.

A family member may come to your office to get information about a relative's mental health or addiction problem, or to discuss his or her own feelings of being overwhelmed. Take the time to provide information, support and encouragement to the family as well as to the person with the problem, so they all get the support they need. Depending on the type of concern, you may want to refer family members for financial advice, legal help, family therapy, individual or couple counselling, or medical services for physical health problems.

While the family member may want to know more about the relative's particular concerns and treatment plan, the client will need to give you permission to have the family member involved in his or her treatment before you can discuss any issues pertaining to the client's care.

While Caroline O'Grady (2005) offers the following tips for working with the families of people with concurrent disorders, the same rules apply for working with families of people with any type of problem:

· *Be respectful* of the vital role they play in their relative's healing, and avoid blaming or criticizing them for their style of coping.
· *Offer support*, whether through referring them for counselling or suggesting ways to take care of themselves and to find their own sources of support.
· *Listen to their feelings and concerns*, acknowledging the difficulties of caring for someone with a significant or chronic problem, and encouraging them to talk about their own feelings and needs.
· *Provide information and education* about how to cope with crises, about the high rate of relapse for people with concurrent disorders and about relevant psychoeducational groups for families.

For information on self-help groups for family members, see page 63.

CHILDREN

Regardless of the type of problem a parent is coping with, children will likely need help to understand and cope themselves: it is important to make sure children are safe and there is care and support for them (including mutual aid groups). They need to be reassured they have not done anything to cause the problems in the family and can't make the problems better by anything they say or do. They also need to know that you and other adults are helping the family member to feel better.

For free, 24-hour telephone support and information, children can contact Kids Help Phone (see Appendix A for details). For information about what kids want to know when a parent dies by suicide, has bipolar disorder, is depressed, has a psychotic disorder or drinks too much, see CAMH's brochures on these topics in Appendix B.

References

Agic, B. (2004). *Culture Counts: Best Practices in Community Education in Mental Health and Addiction with Ethnoracial/Ethnocultural Communities.* Toronto: Centre for Addiction and Mental Health.

Centre for Addiction and Mental Health. (2000). *Alcohol and Drug Treatment in Ontario: A Guide for Helping Professionals.* Toronto: Author.

Centre for Addiction and Mental Health. (2003). *Challenges and Choices: Finding Mental Health Services in Ontario.* Toronto: Author.

Centre for Addiction and Mental Health. (2006). *Navigating Screening Options for Concurrent Disorders.* Toronto: Author.

Centre for Addiction and Mental Health. (2007). *Stigma: Understanding the Impact of Prejudice and Discrimination on People with Mental Health and Substance Use Problems* [Brochure]. Toronto: Author.

Centre for Addiction and Mental Health. (2005). *Problem Gambling: A Guide for Helping Professionals.* Toronto: Centre for Addiction and Mental Health.

Chang, M. & Kelly, A.E. (2007). Patient education: Addressing cultural diversity and health literacy issues. *Urologic Nursing, 27* (5), 411–417.

Cunningham, J.A. (2005). Little use of treatment among problem gamblers. *Psychiatric Services, 56,* 1024–1025. Available: http://psychservices. psychiatryonline.org/cgi/content/full/56/8/1024-a. Accessed June 18, 2008

DiClemente, C.C., Story, M. & Murray, K. (2000). On a roll: The process of initiation and cessation of problem gambling among adolescents. *Journal of Gambling Studies, 16* (2/3), 289–313.

Drug and Alcohol Treatment Information System. (2008). *Substance Abuse Statistical Tables.* Available: www.datis.ca/reports/sa_statistics.html. Accessed August 26, 2008.

Health Canada. (2001). *Best Practices: Concurrent Mental Health and Substance Use Disorders.* Toronto: Author.

Heatherton, T.F., Kozlowski, L.T., Frecker, R.C. & Fagerstrom, K.O. (1991). The Fagerstrom Test for Nicotine Dependence: A revision of the Fagerstrom

Tolerance Questionnaire. *British Journal of Addiction, 86* (9), 1119–1127.

Hester, R.K. & Miller, W.R. (2003). *Handbook of Alcoholism Treatment Approaches: Effective Alternatives*, 3rd ed. Boston, MA: Allyn & Bacon.

Kalman, D., Morissette, S.B. & George, T.P. (2005). Co-morbidity of smoking in patients with psychiatric and substance use disorders. *The American Journal on Addictions*, 14, 106–123.

Kessler, R.C. (1994). The National Comorbidity Survey of the United States. *International Review of Psychiatry, 6*, 365–376.

Kleinman, A. & Benson, P. (2006). Anthropology in the clinic: The problem of cultural competency and how to fix it. *Synergy, 3*, 4–7.

Miller, W.R. & Page, A.C. (1991). Warm turkey: Other routes to abstinence. *Journal of Substance Abuse Treatment, 8*, 227–232.

Miller, W.R. & Sanchez, V.C. (1994). Motivating young adults for treatment and lifestyle change. In G. Howard & P.E. Nathan (Eds.), *Alcohol Use and Misuse by Young Adults*. Notre Dame, IN: University of Notre Dame Press.

O'Grady, C.P. (2005). The impact of concurrent disorders on the family. In W.J.W. Skinner (Ed.), *Treating Concurrent Disorders: A Guide for Counsellors* (pp. 311–330). Toronto: Centre for Addiction and Mental Health.

O'Grady, C.P. & Skinner, W.J.W. (2007). *A Family Guide to Concurrent Disorders*. Toronto: Centre for Addiction and Mental Health.

Prochaska, J. & DiClemente, C. (1984). *The Trans-Theoretical Model: Crossing the Traditional Boundaries of Therapy*. Malabar, FL: Krieger.

Rush, B.R., Bassani, D.G., Urbanoski, K.A. & Castel, S. (2008). Influence of co-occurring mental and substance use disorders on the prevalence of problem gambling in Canada. *Addiction, 103* (11).

Rush, B.R., Urbanoski, K.A., Bassani, D.G., Castel, S., Wild, T.C., Strike, C. et al. (2008, December). Prevalence of co-occurring substance use and other mental disorders in the Canadian population. *Canadian Journal of Psychiatry*.

Sagorsky, L. & Skinner, W. (2005). Using motivational interviewing with clients who have concurrent disorders. In W.J.W. Skinner (Ed.), *Treating*

Concurrent Disorders: A Guide for Counsellors (pp. 85–110). Toronto: Centre for Addiction and Mental Health.

Selby, P. & Herie, M. (in press). Addiction and tobacco use. *Nursing Education Guide: Tobacco Use and Associated Health Risks.*

Skinner, W.J.W., O'Grady, C., Bartha, C. & Parker, C. (2004). *Concurrent Substance Use and Mental Health Disorders: An Information Guide.* Toronto: Centre for Addiction and Mental Health.

Skinner, W. (2005). Preface: Approaching concurrent disorders. In W.J.W. Skinner (Ed.), *Treating Concurrent Disorders: A Guide for Counsellors* (pp. xiii–xix). Toronto: Centre for Addiction and Mental Health.

Substance Abuse and Mental Health Services Agency. (2003). Illness Management and Recovery: Statement on Cultural Competence. Available: http://mentalhealth.samhsa.gov/cmhs/communitysupport/toolkits/illness/ IMRculturalcompetence.asp. Accessed September 4, 2008.

Urbanoski, K.A., Cairney, J., Bassani, D.G. & Rush, B. (2008). Perceived unmet need for mental health care for Canadians with co-occurring mental and substance use disorders. *Psychiatric Services, 59* (3), 283–289.

Wiebe, J., Mun, P. & Kauffman, N. (2006). *Gambling and Problem Gambling in Ontario 2005: Final Report Submitted to the Ontario Problem Gambling Research Centre.* Toronto: Responsible Gambling Council.

Provincial programs

Your first contact: ConnexOntario

Drug and Alcohol Registry of Treatment (DART)
1 800 565-8603
www.dart.on.ca

Ontario Problem Gambling Helpline (OPGH)
1 888 230-3505
www.opgh.on.ca

Mental Health Service Information Ontario (MHSIO)
1 866 531-2600
www.mhsio.on.ca
These services are described on page 55.

Housing, legal and other support services

211 Ontario
211 or 416 397-4636
www.211ontario.ca
Provides information on community, health, social and related services

Community Legal Education Ontario (CLEO)
www.cleo.on.ca
Provides free legal information

Legal Aid Ontario
416 979-1446 or toll-free at 1 800 668-8258
www.legalaid.on.ca
Provides legal aid for people with low incomes or from disadvantaged communities

Ontario Association of Community Care Access Centres
416 750-1720
www.ccac-ont.ca
Provides help in accessing government-funded home care services, long-term care homes, health agencies and other supports in the community

Ontario Self-Help Network (OSHNET)
416 487-4355 or toll-free at 1 888 283-8806
www.selfhelp.on.ca/oshnet.html
Supports the development of self-help groups, networks, organizations and centres in Ontario. OSHNET can link people to self-help groups in their area.

Self-Help Resource Centre
416 487-4355 or toll-free at 1 888 283-8806
www.selfhelp.on.ca
Provides information about and referrals to self-help organizations in your community

Ontario Association of Credit Counselling Services
905 945-5644
www.oaccs.com
Helps people manage debt

Family support

Family Council
416 535-8501 ext. 6499
Provides support, education and advocacy for families of people with mental health problems, addiction or concurrent disorders

Family Association for Mental Health Everywhere (FAME)
416 207-5032
www.fameforfamilies.com
Provides support to families where mental illness is an issue, including individual counselling, support groups and psychoeducation for children

Kids Help Phone
1 800 668-6868
www.kidshelpphone.ca
Provides free phone and online counselling, referral and information for children and youth

Ontario Association for Marriage and Family Therapy
905 936-3338 or 1 800 267-2638
www.oamft.on.ca
Provides referrals to couple and family therapists in your community

Online counselling, support, self-assessment and self-help treatment

The following are interactive websites offering self-assessment tests and support for people with mental health, substance use and gambling problems; the sites are anonymous and confidential but require registration:

· www.alcoholhelpcenter.net
· www.depressioncenter.net
· www.paniccentre.net
· www.smokershelpline.ca
· www.problemgambling.ca.

Problemgambling.ca is one of the most comprehensive sites on gambling, with information for people affected by gambling problems and for helping professionals, including a large number of translated resources. Problemgambling.ca also includes self-assessment and self-help treatment options, and plans to introduce a supportive discussion board and explore other approaches to offering help.

Substance use, mental health, concurrent disorders and problem gambling programs

Anxiety Disorders Association of Ontario
613 729-6761 or toll-free at 1 877 308-3843
www.anxietydisordersontario.ca
Provides information about anxiety and how to find treatment

Assaulted Women's Helpline
416 863-0511 or toll-free at 1 866-863-0511, TTY at 1 866 863-7868
Provides crisis counselling, emotional support, safety planning, guidance around options and referrals as part of a 24-hour crisis line for women in Ontario who have been abused

The Canadian Hearing Society

416 928-2500 or toll-free at 1 877 347-3427
TTY: 416 964-0023 or toll-free at 1 877 347-3429
www.chs.ca/en/counselling.html
Offers assessment and counselling services on mental health and addiction issues for people who are deaf, deafened or hard of hearing, and for their families

Canadian Mental Health Association, Ontario

416 977-5580 or toll-free at 1 800 875-6213
www.ontario.cmha.ca/branches (a branch services database that provides online search of programs at CMHA branches throughout the province)
Provides information and support for people with mental illness, and for their families

Centre for Addiction and Mental Health

Addiction assessment: 416 535-8501 ext. 6616 in Toronto area, or ext. 7062 outside Toronto area or ext. 6071 for medical detox

Addiction clinical consultation service: 416 595-6968 or toll-free at 1 888-720-ACCS/2227 (information, advice and professional support to clinicians on medical complications of alcohol and other drug use, drug interactions, concurrent disorders etc.)

General mental health assessment: 416 979-6878

Problem Gambling Service: 416 599-1322 or toll-free at 1 888 647-4414

www.camh.net

A teaching and research hospital dedicated to assessment and treatment of people with mental health and/or addiction problems, and research and education on these issues

Compulsive Gamblers Hub

www.cghub.homestead.com
An Internet self-help group based on Gamblers Anonymous

Gamb-ling: Niagara Multilingual Prevention/Education Problem Gambling Program
905 378-4647 ext. 63849
www.gamb-ling.com

Provides multilingual problem gambling information, awareness and prevention for diverse ethnocultural communities in the Niagara region

Mood Disorders Association of Ontario
416 486-8046 or toll-free at 1 888 486-8236
www.mooddisorders.on.ca
Provides information and support to people with depression or bipolar disorder, and to their families; peer support offered by phone and support groups available

National Native Alcohol and Drug Abuse Program (NNADAP)
www.hc-sc.gc.ca/fnih-spni/substan/ads/nnadap-pnlaada_e.html
Helps First Nations and Inuit communities set up and operate substance use programs for people on reserves

Schizophrenia & Substance Use
www.schizophreniaandsubstanceuse.ca
Part of a project by the Schizophrenia Society of Canada that provides information for clients, families and service providers on the link between these concurrent disorders

Schizophrenia Society of Ontario
416 449-6830 or toll-free at 1 800 449-6367
www.schizophrenia.on.ca
Provides support and education to families of people with schizophrenia

Self-Help Resource Centre
416 487-4355 or toll-free at 1 888 283-8806
www.selfhelp.on.ca
Increases awareness of self-help / mutual aid and facilitates the growth and development of self-help groups, networks and resources; this includes providing information and offering workshops on a variety of topics (e.g., on

starting a self-help group, integrating self-help strategies at work, facilitating groups). It also has a searchable database for finding a group in Ontario.

Smoker's Helpline
1 877 513-5333
www.smokershelpline.ca
Provides phone and online support to help people quit smoking

YMCA Youth Gambling Program
1 877-525-5515 ext. 4039
www.ymcatoronto.org/gambling
A free service offering help in 19 communities to children and youth aged eight to 24 who are coping with potentially addictive behaviours related to gambling

CAMH resources and publications

Further information about mental health, substance use and problem gambling is available from CAMH as follows:

CAMH McLaughlin Information Centre
Automated response line 24 hours a day; staffed between 9:00 a.m. and 9:00 p.m., seven days a week, except on statutory holidays

416 595-6111 or toll-free at 1 800 463-6273

CAMH Education
www.camh.net/education/index.html

CAMH Library
416 535 8501 ext. 6991 (Russell St. site) or ext. 2158 (Queen St. site)

www.camh.net/About_Addiction_Mental_Health/CAMH_Library/index.html

CAMH Provincial Services
System planning, local education and training, project consulting through local regional staff

www.camh.net/About_CAMH/Contact_us/index.html

CAMH Publications

416 595-6059 or toll-free at 1 800 661-1111

www.camh.net/publications

To order the following publications, or to receive a listing of other CAMH products, please contact the Sales and Distribution department:

416 595-6059 or toll-free at 1 800 661-1111
publications@camh.net.

You can also view a description of each of these CAMH publications on the website at www.camh.net (click the "Publications" link). Many can be downloaded, either partially or in their entirety.

Substance use

Brands, B., Sproule, B. & Marshman, J. (Eds.). (1998). *Drugs and Drug Abuse.*

Centre for Addiction and Mental Health. (2003). *Is It Safe for My Baby? Risks and Recommendations for the Use of Medication, Alcohol, Tobacco and Other Drugs during Pregnancy and Breastfeeding.*

Centre for Addiction and Mental Health and Motherisk. (2007). *Exposure to Psychotropic Medications and Other Substances during Pregnancy and Lactation: A Handbook for Health Care Providers.*

Centre for Addiction and Mental Health. (nd). *Do You Know…* Pamphlet series. Toronto: Author.

Harrison, S. & Carver, V. (Eds.). (2004). *Alcohol & Drug Problems: A Practical Guide for Counsellors* (3rd ed.)

Herie, M., Godden, T., Shenfeld, J. & Kelly, C. (2007). *Addiction: An Information Guide.*

Poole, N. & Greaves, L. (Eds.). (2007). *Highs and Lows: Canadian Perspectives on Women and Substance Use.*

Sanchez-Craig, M. (1995). *DrinkWise: How to Quit Drinking or Cut Down.*

Concurrent disorders

O'Grady, C.P. & Skinner, W.J.W. (2007). *A Family Guide to Concurrent Disorders.*

Skinner, W.J.W. (Ed.). (2005). *Treating Concurrent Disorders: A Guide for Counsellors.*

Skinner, W.J.W., O'Grady, C.P., Bartha, C. & Parker, C. (2004). *Concurrent Substance Use and Mental Health Disorders: An Information Guide.*

Problem gambling

Centre for Addiction and Mental Health. (2004a). *Problem Gambling: A Guide for Families.*

Centre for Addiction and Mental Health. (2004b). *Problem Gambling: A Guide for Financial Counsellors.*

Centre for Addiction and Mental Health. (2004c). *Problem Gambling: The Issues, the Options.*

Centre for Addiction and Mental Health. (2005). *Problem Gambling: A Guide for Helping Professionals.*

For children

Centre for Addiction and Mental Health. (2002). *Can I Catch It Like a Cold? A Story to Help Children Understand a Parent's Depression.*

Centre for Addiction and Mental Health. *What kids want to know...* brochure series: When a parent dies by suicide (2004), When a parent has bipolar disorder (2003), When a parent drinks too much alcohol (2005), When a parent has experienced psychosis (2005), When a parent is depressed (2003).

Centre for Addiction and Mental Health. (2005). *Wishes and Worries: A Story to Help Children Understand a Parent Who Drinks Too Much Alcohol.*

Working with special populations

Barankin, T. & Khanlou, N. (2007). *Growing Up Resilient: Ways to Build Resilience in Children and Youth.*

Barbara, A.M., Chaim, G. & Doctor, F. (2007). *Asking the Right Questions 2: Talking with Clients about Sexual Orientation and Gender Identity in Mental Health, Counselling and Addiction Settings.*

CAMH Healthy Aging Project. (2008). *Improving Our Response to Older Adults with Substance Use, Mental Health and Gambling Problems: A Guide for Supervisors, Managers and Clinical Staff.*

Centre for Addiction and Mental Health. (2004). *Youth & Drugs and Mental Health: A Resource for Professionals.*

Guruge, S. & Collins, E. (2008). *Working with Immigrant Women: Issues and Strategies for Mental Health Professionals.*

Haskell, L. (2001). *Bridging Responses: A Front-Line Worker's Guide to Supporting Women Who Have Post-Traumatic Stress.*

Wolfe. D.A. (Ed.). (2007). *Acting Out: Understanding and Reducing Aggressive Behaviour in Children and Youth.*